WHAT
CHRISTIANS
BELIEVE

Copyright © 1984 Lion Publishing

Published by
Lion Publishing plc
Icknield Way, Tring, Herts, England
ISBN 0 85648 566 7
Lion Publishing Corporation
10885 Textile Road, Belleville, Michigan 48111, USA
ISBN 0 85648 566 7
Albatross Books
PO Box 320, Sutherland, NSW 2232, Australia
ISBN 0 86760 492 1

First edition 1984
Reprinted 1984
Reprinted 1985 (twice)

British Library Cataloguing in Publication Data

Balchin, J.F.
    What Christians believe.—(Lion manuals; 4)
    1. Faith
    I. Title
    201   BT771.2
    ISBN 0 85648 566 7

Library of Congress Cataloging in Publication Data

Balchin, John F., 1937–
    What Christians believe.
    1. Theology, Doctrinal—Popular works. I. Title.
BT77.B29 1984   230   83-26570
ISBN 0 85648 566 7

Phototypesetting by Parkway Group, London and Abingdon
Printed in Yugoslavia by Mladinska Knjiga Printing House

John Balchin

WHAT CHRISTIANS BELIEVE

A LION MANUAL
Tring · Belleville · Sydney

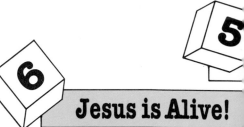
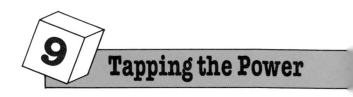
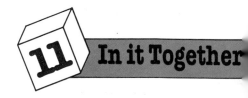

CONTENTS

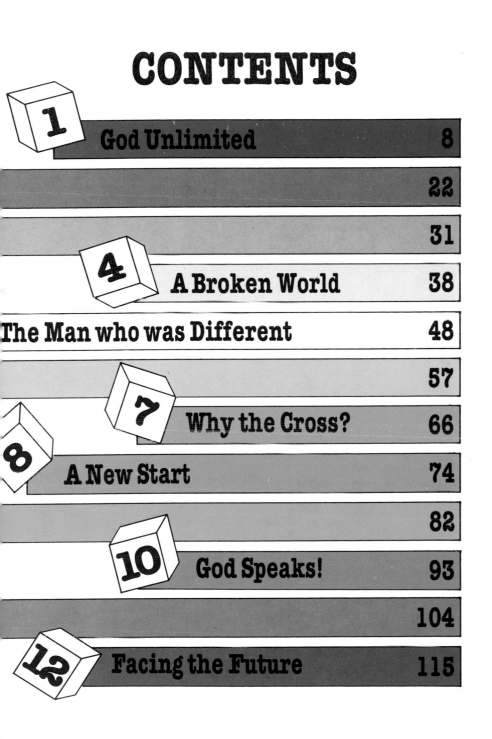

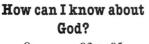

GOD
UNLIMITED

Take a flower, watch a sunset, look up at the stars, look into a human face and you are where the Christian faith begins. For the Bible opens with God making everything around us, mighty mountains or tiny blades of grass, all coming as if from his drawing board. There was nothing there before. It was all called into being and life by the Creator who is also responsible for keeping it running and supplied. This is the God of the Bible.

The writers of the Bible assumed that anyone, seeing the amazing variety and intricacy of the universe, must conclude that someone made it and keeps it going. They believed it was obvious that behind the universe's beautiful design and delicately balanced laws was an intelligence and energy far greater than anything we can grasp.

❝Ever since God created the world, his invisible qualities, both his eternal power and his divine nature, have been clearly seen; they are perceived in the things God has made.❞

Paul

The Bible writers were so sure of this that they never went about proving God's existence as others have tried to since. The Bible begins by stating it, and one writer even claimed that only fools could say 'there is no God'.

Why doesn't everybody see it, then? The Bible tells us that the evidence is there in plenty, but that people simply don't want to know! There is a popular idea that men and women have always been looking for God, gradually refining their ideas about him. But the Bible turns this upside down. Instead it tells us that we run away from God, preferring to worship other, substitute gods. God has to seek after men and women, showing them, sometimes against their will, what he is really like.

Who is this God?

It's all very well talking about God – but what do we mean by the word? The Bible gives us some basic pointers to who God is. Jesus once said to his followers, 'God is Spirit'. He was using a well-known picture about God. When the Jewish people wanted to describe God who they could not see, but who could do great and powerful things, they thought of the wind bending the trees or whipping up the waves. That is what 'spirit' really means. But it can equally be used for a person's breath. And as breathing means living, it carries the idea of life-giving power.

The Bible also tells us that God is . . .
● **Invisible.** We cannot see him although he is there all the time. This

Can we know that God exists?

The nearest the Bible comes to a 'proof' of God is to point us towards the structure and order of the universe, and also to the way human beings behave.

It has often been argued that there are good reasons to say there is a God, because of . . .

● the existence of the world;
● the design of the universe;
● the way human beings are made;
● the need we have for a purpose and value in life;
● the fact that everybody worships something;
● the very idea of perfection in an imperfect world.

All these are attempts to answer the why, what and how of the universe, and to solve something of the riddle of life itself. A thief who forgets to wear gloves gives himself away by the fingerprints he leaves behind. In the same way, God 'gives himself away' by leaving his fingerprints all over his creation. In these ways many people have groped towards someone or something standing behind the creation as we see it. The Bible provides an end to their search, because it tells us that the person who made everything is a living, loving God whom we can know as our Father.

Soviet cosmonauts in the 1960s said that they did not see God while in space. But some of the American astronauts experienced the wonder of God's creation in space and on the moon. A sense of the mystery of the universe, of something beyond our limited lives, can come to those who are ready to look for it.

The Christian faith is a personal faith. It is about a God who knows us inside out, and who wants us to know him.

means that we cannot make accurate pictures or images of him.
● **A person.** He is not just power, energy or a cosmic force. We cannot talk with a force – but we can talk with the God of the Bible.
● **Distinct from what he made.** Some people believe that everything that exists is part of God. But the Bible tells us that God stands over and above the universe.
● **Involved in the affairs of our world, keeping it running.** He is not distant or remote. He did not make the world and then kick it into space and forget it. He cares for what he created.

We can know God

The Christian God is not just an idea or a thing. He's a person, and that means that we can know him just as we know other persons. As individuals, we have our own personalities, make decisions, and live our own lives. In the Bible, God too acts and thinks – and he has personality. He decided to make the world in the first place, and later on it was he who took the first step when it came to meeting with people.

Nor is he a cold or remote being. We're told that he can feel; that he can be

The universe, with its bewildering size and minute detail, gives us vital clues about the character of the God who made it all.

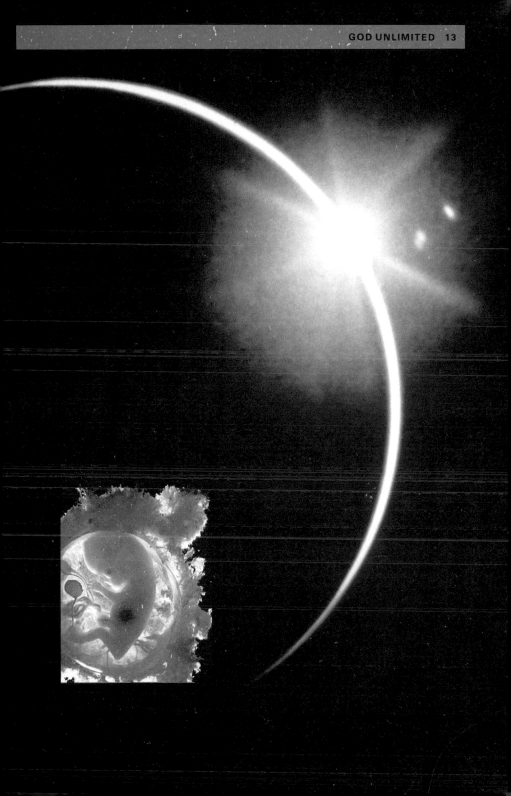

hurt; that he can love and that he can grieve. That is why right and wrong matter to him, and why his moral laws are not impersonal rules like the law of gravity. Disregard them and we personally insult him.

But perhaps the most important side to God's nature from our viewpoint is that he goes out of his way to have personal relationships with men and women. He wants us to know and love him, and at the same time he wants to help us in the lives we lead. The great theme running through the Bible and lying behind the Christian message is just how this can be possible.

Only one God

The people of the Bible were not the only ones to worship something, any more than Christians are today. Most men and women in all times and places have worshipped something, whether it was the spirit of some river or mountain, or their dead ancestors, or a variety of mythical gods and goddesses, or even some system or ideology like Communism. **God's people had to learn that there was one, and only one, legitimate God who could be rightly worshipped.** The people of Israel were told: 'The Lord – and the Lord alone – is our God.' Over against the paganism and idolatry of the nations round about them, they had to be taught – sometimes the hard way – that there was only one God worthy of the name.

We see this in the way in which the Old Testament prophets belittled the gods of other peoples, and poured scorn on their idolatry as something powerless and futile. In fact, later on, the apostle Paul saw paganism as one of the Devil's disguises, leading men and women astray. When people became Christians, they turned away from worshipping anything and everything else, and put their trust in the one, true God.

Who keeps it all going?

We can learn a good deal about God from the fact that he keeps the universe running. That in itself tells us how great he is.

**❝Look up at the sky!
Who created the stars you see?
The one who leads them out
like an army,
he knows how many there are
and calls each one by name!
His power is so great –
not one of them is ever missing!❞**

Isaiah

The universe also tells us about God's intelligence. Our most advanced scientists are still only beginning to discover what God put there in the first place. They are continually baffled by the way in which everything holds together and runs so smoothly. The Bible tells us that God knows every detail perfectly.

But creation would be overpowering were it not for the fact that God also looks after what he has made. The vast universe can be a terrifying and awesome place, but God also made a beautiful and pleasant world where life could flourish. This was something that Jesus reminded his disciples about. He told them that as God feeds the sparrows and clothes the hillside flowers in all their beauty, so too he takes care of us.

The amazing thing is that God goes on looking after us whether we trust him or not. He doesn't stop supplying our needs even though we may have turned our backs on him. There are so many things which we take for granted: life itself, health, food, homes and human love; peace, law and order, human rights; joy and pleasures, the beauty that thrills us, the spectacular views that awe us. **It's all still there for us whether we gratefully**

Do all religions lead to God?

In these days, when many societies are racially mixed, Christians often find themselves living alongside people whose beliefs are very different from their own. What about that Muslim next door, or the Sikh we meet each day at work? Are their religions simply alternative routes to God? What is the Christian's attitude to other faiths?

The history and beliefs of other religions are just as distinctive as those of Christianity. Sometimes they enshrine lofty ideals; sometimes they propose answers to the mysteries of life; sometimes they reflect the harsh and cruel environment in which men and women have to exist. Most, like the Christian faith, would claim to be exclusive. For example, you cannot be a Muslim and a Hindu. This is because, whereas all religions do have something in common, each one is very different when it comes to what people actually believe. The gods of Hinduism or the African religions, or even Islam where only one god is worshipped are not the same, any more than they are the same as the God of the Bible. Equally, the ways in which people are expected to live and

worship in various religions are very different, and those who are committed to another faith would tell you so without apology. So, in this sense, it would be a fallacy to say that all religions lead to the same goal. They never claim to.

What do they have in common then? From a Christian point of view, the world religions tell us more about mankind than they do about God. They remind us that men and women have always needed something bigger than themselves to worship and serve. They reflect a longing, built into human nature by our Creator, for a spiritual dimension to life. In that respect, the religions which have been imported into the west from the east challenge our godless materialism, while the zeal with which others pursue their faith is often a rebuke to half-hearted Christians who might claim they know better.

The Christian respects the views of those who disagree with him. After all, in the past it has been Christians who have fought for religious toleration for all people. Yet at the same time Christians maintain that in Christ we have God's unique way of getting right with him.

"You have set the earth firmly on its foundations,
   and it will never be moved. . .
You make springs flow in the valleys,
   and rivers run between the hills.
They provide water for the wild animals;
   there the wild donkeys quench their thirst.
In the trees nearby, the birds make their nests and sing.
From the sky you send rain on the hills,
   and the earth is filled with your blessings.
You make grass grow for the cattle and plants for man to use,
so that he can grow his crops and produce wine to make him happy,
   olive-oil to make him cheerful, and bread to give him strength.**"**

Psalm 104

serve God or not. God goes on caring for us in spite of ourselves.

God is in control

The Bible authors were quite sure that God not only made the world, but that he was also master of it and everything that happened in it.

> **❝The Lord is a mighty God, a mighty king over all the gods. He rules over the whole earth, from the deepest caves to the highest hills. He rules over the sea, which he made; the land also, which he himself formed.❞** Psalm 95

This means that in the end God will get his way. As we read the daily bad news in our newspapers, it can be hard to believe that God is really in control. But Christians believe that God is often able to bring good out of even the most painful events, and that ultimately his goodness will be victorious over evil. Even when Jesus was betrayed and crucified, his followers claimed that it had all happened as part of God's own plan. They spoke about Jesus' death as the **good news** of what God had done.

But although God is in overall control of our world, this does not mean that we are just puppets dancing at the end of strings held by him. He made us with the freedom to choose for ourselves – even though it means that we choose to rebel against him. The Bible tells us that we are completely responsible for what we do. But at the same time it says that God works out what he wants in his own way.

God is greater than we can imagine. He knows about everything that happens and is in overall control of our world.

God unlimited

The Bible shows us that God is more than just a force behind the universe – he is also a person. But it is wrong to think of him simply as a person like ourselves. In many ways he is more than a person:

● **He is self-contained.** He is not limited by anyone or anything else. By contrast, we are dependent on him and on other people. He depends on no one.

● **He is eternal.** He is above and beyond time. He is always the same. He does not change or grow old as we do.

● **He is everywhere.** He is not limited by space or distance. He is the very ground of what we are while also being at the farthest star.

● **He knows everything.** God has not had to learn anything. He even knows the future before it happens.

● **He can do anything** he wants, whenever he wants to do it. He is not limited by weakness as we are.

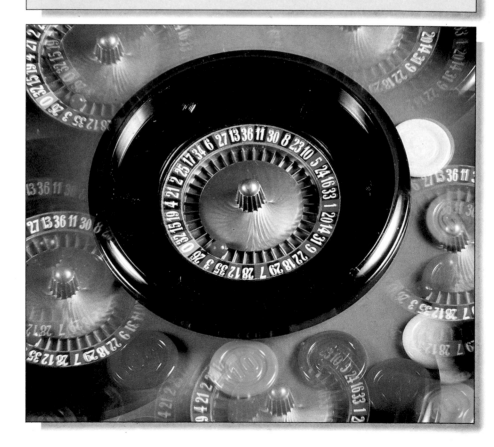

This often causes problems for us because we cannot see how God's control and our free wills can run together. But this is because we don't see things from his point of view. Like a master chess player, God has all his moves, and ours, worked out before they take place. It was no problem for the Bible's authors. They quite clearly tell us that we are completely responsible for what we do, but at the same time they also say most strongly that God works out what he wants in his own way.

Not just chance

Many people today believe that the universe fell together by chance, and that there is no purpose behind it. If that is so, our lives also must be just as random and meaningless – and they often are.

We didn't ask to be born into a world where people are just so many pawns in a game without rules, or cogs in a machine which is running wild. For many people life *is* totally meaningless – and it makes them feel horribly afraid. They fall sick, they're made redundant, their marriages turn sour, they live under the shadow of the Bomb – and there's nothing they can do about it. No wonder so many are tempted to end it all, for life seems to be going nowhere, and death seems to be a welcome relief.

But the law and order that we see all around us can give us real hope, and stop us from coming to that depressing conclusion. Take a radio telescope and scan the outer reaches of space – or take an electron microscope and explore that hidden world far beyond the range of sight – and everywhere you look you will find order and design. Without it science would be impossible – and life would be intolerable. Everything would be so unsure and uncertain that daily living would be a nightmare.

But the world isn't like that. The ground is solid; water is wet; the air is breathable; what we drop falls; light shines, and so on. We make a thousand assumptions like these every day. If we could not, it would be like trying to live in a hall of distorting mirrors.

The order, design and law we see in the world tell us that God is not a haphazard, disorganized Creator who either forgets what he has done, or who makes things up as he goes along. They tell us that he is a God of purpose who plans for what he has made.

And if this is true for stars or atoms, it encourages us to believe that it can also be true for human lives or for the history of the world. As we shall see, when we get to know this God, we can find meaning and purpose in life for ourselves.

Christians believe that life on earth is more than just the result of chance. Life was designed and brought into being by God.

WHO IS GOD?

What do we conjure up in our minds when we think about God? How do we imagine him? Is he some vague, undefined Force? Is he some kind of super-policeman always checking up on us? Is he an alien from outer space? Or the frightening power of uncontrollable nature? Or do we imagine him as an old man with a long beard who wearily contemplates a wayward world from somewhere up above the clouds? Fortunately we're not left to make up our own minds, because God has gone out of his way to show us what he's like. Over many years and in a variety of ways he made himself known to people. We can know what kind of God he is.

The Holy One

As we have seen, God is far above and beyond our human weakness. This is something of what the Bible authors meant when they said that God was 'holy'. They meant that he was utterly separate, wholly other, far above the human race. He was surrounded by mystery which made them hold their breath. He was their God who wanted to have dealings with them, and yet they knew that when they came into touch with him, they were right out of their depth. They couldn't be flippant about him or take his name lightly. They took great care in approaching him, and avoided all casualness when they worshipped him.

This was something they had to learn. He gave them a highly elaborate ritual involving priests and sacrifices for their worship. Without these safeguards, they didn't dare come too near. It was like handling high voltage electricity. **After all, you can't play around with the vast energy that brought the universe into being and which keeps it going – and get away with it.**

But there was another meaning to this word 'holy'. God showed the people of the Old Testament that he had fixed standards for daily living which they always failed to live up to. He called them to live **holy** lives – that is, lives free from evil and which pleased him. He wanted them to be holy like himself.

Absolutely straight

That's what the Bible means by the word 'righteous'. There are agreed standards for building safe houses, and so too God sets standards for our lives which are right and true. You know where you are with him. He doesn't demand one thing one day and another the next. This is why God gave us laws like the Ten Commandments. They are clear instructions for daily living. They tell us what is right and what is wrong; what pleases God, and what he hates.

They also show us how different from God we are. He is light compared with our moral darkness. He is purity in contrast with our spiritual dirtiness.

A just judge

Because of who he is, God alone is qualified to judge mankind, and the Bible tells us that one day he will. If we break one of the natural laws built into the fabric of the universe, we suffer for it. If we defy the law of gravity by foolishly stepping off a cliff, we get what we deserve at the bottom! In a similar way, we can't play around with God's moral laws. If we do not reap the results in this life, the Bible tells us that there will be a final reckoning.

None of us likes this idea – we would prefer God to close his eyes to the things we do wrong. But Christians believe God is a just God. Imagine how terrifying it would be to live with an unjust God! So we must be prepared to face his justice. We ask for as much when we demand our rights. One day God will make sure that we get them. The sins and wickednesses of the human race will be rewarded. The sufferings and injustices will be redressed – because God is just.

What is more, because we are dealing with a person and not just a system, to break God's laws is to rebel against God. The crimes and injustices that we see in life often deeply upset and anger us. And in the same way, our rebellion grieves and angers God. To have a God who is straight and true can be either reassuring or disturbing depending on how we live.

Right and wrong

There are plenty of people who are all at sea when it comes to right and wrong. Social standards seem to change so quickly that what was wrong yesterday seems OK today. Everybody seems to be doing their own thing. Who's to say what's right or what's wrong?

But it isn't quite like that. If there is no such thing as right or wrong, why is it that certain crimes and atrocities we read about in the papers or see on TV make us angry or disturbed? Most people do have some standards which they set for themselves. There are things they wouldn't do, and there are things that they will do. Every society also sets certain limits when it comes to people's behaviour, because no government could ever afford to let people do anything they wanted to.

But where do we get all these standards from? The Bible tells us that God has built into us a sensitivity to evil. Our consciences respond to evil as a mine-detector finds dangerous explosives. What's more, God has shown us quite plainly (in the Bible) what is right and what is wrong.

The Bible tells us that right is what God wants, and that wrong is what he hates. It says that because God is good, so too he expects us to be good. This is something which we can see in God's Old Testament laws. The Ten Commandments are the best known:

1 Worship no god but me.
2 Do not make yourselves images of anything . . . do not bow down to any idol or worship it.
3 Do not use my name for evil purposes.
4 Observe the sabbath day and keep it holy.
5 Respect your father and mother.
6 Do not commit murder.
7 Do not commit adultery.
8 Do not steal.
9 Do not accuse anyone falsely.
10 Do not desire another person's possessions.

Jesus was once asked what he thought God's greatest commandment was. He replied: 'Love the Lord your God with all your heart, with all your soul, and with all your mind.' And then he added that the second most important commandment was similar: 'Love your neighbour as you love yourself.'

It is by God's laws that we test our standards and our behaviour. Like a carpenter shaping up a piece of wood, God sets the straight edge of his law against our lives.

Agape – a word for loving

The word 'love' today is like a piece of elastic. It is pulled and stretched in all directions. Love is what happens between two people on the cinema screen when they kiss in the sunset. Love is something we fall into – and fall out of. We can even 'make' love. The word love is often very misused. So what does it mean to say that God loves us and that we can love him?

The writers of the New Testament had the same dilemma when they came to use the word love. There were several words in the Greek language they could have used, but most had been spoiled by misuse. One word, *eros*, had been so widely used for sexual love that it had come simply to mean 'lust'.

The word which had the least bad overtones was *agape* (pronounced agapay), and this word came into its own in the New Testament. It became the favourite word when it came to speaking about God's love for the world, our love for God, or even our love for one another.

God loved us enough to send Jesus to die for us on the cross. This filled the word *agape* with new meaning. It came to mean loving the unattractive and undeserving. It means reconciliation with old enemies, welcoming them open-heartedly. Agape is more than just the nice feeling that modern love often is. It means to be committed to loving and caring for the other person, no matter what.

Because of the depth of meaning in *agape*, it has become an ideal word for Christians to use, especially in showing how God's love leaps over racial, sexual and social barriers. And if asked why Christians love like this, the answer is that this is the way in which God loves them.

God of the downtrodden

What must it be like living – as many have to – in a society where there's no hope of getting justice? Where, in spite of your innocence, your rights are taken away, you are injured and hurt, and no one cares? Where the judge is bent and the lawyers have been bribed and the jury threatened? You haven't a hope in a system like that.

That's why over the years the oppressed and the falsely accused, the enslaved and the dispossessed have turned to the just God of the Bible for their rights and for their vindication. And that's why Christians, who believe in that God, have often been in the forefront of legal reform, standing up for what is right and just.

The genuine article

The Bible writers often talked about their God as the true God, quite unlike the false gods of the surrounding nations. He was the only real God, who could actually do things for his people. They also meant that he is constant and reliable, and that you can trust him to fulfil his promises. For God never contradicts himself or goes back on his word. That is one of the reasons why we can take what the Bible says as being true.

In the Old Testament, God's people demonstrated this all through their history. He had made a special agreement (or 'covenant') with them, an agreement which they repeatedly broke. God often allowed them to suffer for their wrongdoing, but he did not forget that he had promised to be their God. Again and again he stepped into their tangled affairs to rescue them, and to bring them back into line. **Something which runs right through the Christian message is that God is good to us in** spite of ourselves – because he is true to himself.

God is love

One of the most wonderful truths in the whole Bible, which is at the very heart of what Christians believe, is that this great and holy God loves men and women. If we didn't know this, there is a lot about him that we would fear and dread – his majesty, his purity, his power, his justice. But along with terms like these, the Bible uses a cluster of warm, human words which tell us that God has a loving heart.

He loves us in the same way that a parent loves his child, or as a husband loves his wife. He sympathizes with our weakness; he has compassion on us because we are lost. He breaks his heart over people whose lives are a mess. He goes out of his way to meet the needs of the poor, the troubled, the sad and the lonely.

We can see this in the way that he looked after the Jewish people – even though they rebelled against him. We can see this in the promises he has made to be close to us in our difficulties, and to guide the direction of our lives. We can see this most of all in the fact that he sent Jesus, his only Son, to die for us.

❝This is what love is: it is not that we have loved God, but that he loved us and sent his Son to be the means by which our sins are forgiven. ❞
John

All you need is love . . .

. . . Well, not quite all, but we would have a pretty thin time without it. Psychologists tell us that if a child is to

Isn't the Bible full of don'ts?

There seem to be plenty of things that the Bible tells us we mustn't do. Isn't God's law just a bit restrictive and kill-joy? Doesn't it make God seem rather like a policeman who is forever looking over our shoulders and stopping us doing what we want to?

It is true to say that the Bible contains laws – some of which warn us against doing certain things. But with many of these laws it's easy to see that they were given for our own good and for the good of other people. They tell us not to lie to, or deceive, others. They forbid discriminating against people of a different race. God gives us rules to stop us hurting ourselves – and to protect the community.

But the Bible isn't simply a collection of 'do nots'. One of its great themes is that by knowing God we can be set free from wrong behaviour to do what is right. Of course, too many rules can lead to slavery. But **some** rules are important for freedom. Think about learning to play the piano. It's only when someone learns and follows the 'rules' of piano-playing that he is then free to enjoy playing music. God's laws are meant to work in the same way.

---

develop normally, it needs a secure, loving home. Teenagers long for love as their emotions tell them that life was made to be shared. Married couples experience the deep fulfilment which comes from loving and being loved. Families thrive on it. Good communities offer that warm sense of belonging which is love. The elderly find meaning in their lives when they know that someone cares. We all need love and loving.

That is why it is such a tragedy that we live in a love-starved world. Where unwanted and neglected children are a fact of life. Where the emotions of the young are exploited. Where husbands and wives are at loggerheads. Where neighbours live in hate. Where racial and sectarian violence blast community life.

Where the poor, the sick, the elderly, the feeble and the handicapped can be tossed aside.

Thank God that he not only has enough love to fill the empty places in our hearts and lives, but that he also teaches us to love people we would normally not bother with.

God the shepherd

King David started life as a shepherd boy caring for his sheep on the hills around Bethlehem. He drew on his experience as a shepherd when he described the way God had dealt with him. He struck the balance beautifully between God's care and God's discipline like this:

The Lord is my shepherd; I have everything I need.
He lets me rest in fields of green grass
    and leads me to quiet pools of fresh water.
He gives me new strength.
    He guides me in the right paths, as he has promised.
Even if I go through the deepest darkness,
    I will not be afraid, Lord, for you are with me.
Your shepherd's rod and staff protect me.

You prepare a banquet for me, where all my enemies can see me;
you welcome me as an honoured guest and fill my cup to the brim.
I know that your goodness and love will be with me all my life;
    and your house will be my home as long as I live. **99** Psalm 23

Benevolent grandfather?

Love is such an elastic word that it can mean many different things. Some people think of God's love in a soft, indulgent way. They see him as a rather senile old man, ladling out favours indiscriminately to one and all. They assume that it doesn't really matter what you believe or how you live, because God's love can cope with all that, and bring everyone safely home at last.

But real love isn't like that, especially when it's the love of a holy God. Love wants the very best for the person loved. Loving parents do not give their children everything they ask for. Because they want the best for them they will withold some things, and sometimes positively discipline their children. Good parents teach their children the difference between right and wrong, and keep them to it when they step out of line.

It is because God is holy as well as loving that he goes about establishing right where there is wrong and justice where there is wickedness. He works to reverse the trend of evil in human lives.

That is why the Bible's picture of God is that of a wise, kind Father, who has high ambitions for us if we are his children – not a weak, indulgent parent who couldn't care less. He wants the best and the highest for us. He wants us to share something of his family likeness.

In order to do that, he had to devise a way to help us which, at one and the same time, showed just how serious our wrongdoing was, and just how great his love for us was. That is what the cross, the central symbol of the Christian faith, is all about.

A God who goes looking

One of the distinctive things Jesus taught about God was that he didn't wait for

Abba

When Jesus prayed, he used a word his fellow-Jews would never have dared to use of God. He called him 'Abba' which, in Jesus' mother-tongue, Aramaic, was almost like saying 'Daddy'. It was what Jewish boys and girls called their dads in those days. It was daring, it was shocking – but it summed up the close, intimate relationship he had with God.

But then he turned to his disciples and taught them to use it too! Not everyone can speak of God in this way. Only in the very broadest sense of being God's creatures are we all God's children. But those people whose lives are committed to Jesus can know the same sort of close, deep bond with the God who cares for us in the same way that we care for our youngsters.

people to come to him. He went to them where they were. He was like a shepherd who had lost one sheep – and who went out looking for it. He was like a woman who had lost a coin in her house – and who turned the place upside down until she found it.

In the same way, God loves people so much that he makes the first move. We often only help people when we think they deserve it. But the Bible tells us that God came to our rescue when we had deliberately turned our backs on him. Those who come to know God soon realize that long before they began to think about him, he came after them, showing them the way back.

That's the kind of God we're dealing with: a God who **wants** people to be right with him, and to experience for themselves everything he can do for them.

PEOPLE ARE SPECIAL

Our lives and what goes on in them are important and seem big to us. But we can often get the feeling that really we're tiny and powerless – especially when we're up against the bigness of the world we live in. When world leaders manoeuvre the world towards war, we are just pieces pushed around in an international game. When the astronomers start talking about the vast, unimaginable distances between the galaxies in our universe – measured in terms of how far light will travel in **years** – what are we but microscopic specks, feebly crawling over the surface of an insignificant golf ball of a planet? Why do we have the cheek to think that as human beings we're somehow different or special?

Lost in space?

One writer in the Bible also experienced this sense of being lost in a big world. But he found a reason for his own significance because of what God had done:

66 **When I look at the sky, which you have made,**
  at the moon and the stars, which you set in their places –
what is man, that you think of him; mere man, that you care for him?
Yet you made him inferior only to yourself;
  you crowned him with glory and honour.
You appointed him ruler over everything you made;
  you placed him over all creation:
  sheep and cattle, and the wild animals too;
  the birds and the fish, and the creatures of the seas.
O Lord, our Lord,
  your greatness is seen in all the world! 99
Psalm 8

People like God?

The very first chapter of the Bible tells us that God made us 'in his own image'. We are like God. Like a mirror, we reflect something of what God is himself.

Most people would protest that human beings aren't very godlike in many of the things they do. This is true, and there's a very good reason for this as we shall see. But in other ways, the Bible words still apply.

● **Personally – we are individuals in our own right.** We have wills and minds of our own. We think, feel, decide and act for ourselves. Just as God can say 'I', so can we. That's why we get so heated about our rights and freedoms. Even in societies which have been schooled to think that the state always has the last say, people look for freedom of expression and belief. Freedom, that is, to be themselves . . . because that's how God made them.

● **Morally – we all know something about right and wrong.** We all know what it means to have moral rules – and

God made people to enjoy creativity. We can follow in the footsteps of the Creator God.

to suffer from that strange feeling we call 'conscience' when we break them. This is just as true for people who have never read the Bible. It's universal. Standards and laws differ from place to place and from time to time, but there are always *some* standards and laws. Even crooks have their own code of behaving!

The Bible tells us that, in the beginning, there was more to it than this. God made everything good, so the first people were actually like him morally – they were holy and loving and all the rest. That was something they lost, but the awareness of right and wrong still remains.

● **Socially – we need one another,** in fact we can have a special kind of relationship with one another – and with God – which we call a **personal** relationship. We can't have this relationship with things. I don't chat to my cabbages or strike up a friendship with my chair. That's why people living on their own can feel so desperately lonely. We were made for society, living and loving and sharing together. The close, deep bond of marriage is only one part of God's plan to meet this need.

● **Religiously – we need to worship.** People are religious. If man is an animal then he's a most peculiar kind of animal because he wants to worship something outside himself. People everywhere want something greater than this world or this life can offer. World-wide religion tells us that. Even modern, secular people who say they have no need for God, have to fill the God-shaped gap in their lives with something. It might be business,

money, pleasure, politics, a secure house and home, or ambition. But none of these things will do. God made us for **himself.**

● **Purposefully – we need direction in life.** Either we do have a sense of purpose, or at least we feel the need for purpose in our lives. God did not make men and women and turn them loose. He gave them something to do. That's why unemployment can be so soul-destroying. That's why one of the deepest problems our generation faces is loss of purpose and loss of nerve – because our generation has lost God.

❝You have made us for yourself, and our hearts are restless till they find their rest in you.❞
Augustine

Taking charge

At the very beginning of the Bible, when God first made people, he gave them control over everything else he had made. In spite of the fact that we have made a mess of things, our long history of exploration, discovery, invention and design is the way in which this has worked out. Some of our achievements have been quite remarkable.

Think about the technology involved in putting a man on the moon, or the engineering skills required to put up our huge buildings and bridges, or the musical expertise behind the writing – and the playing – of a single symphony. Think about everything people have done in the realms of art and science, in physics and medicine, literature and law, politics and philosophy and all the rest, and you will begin to realize that the human being is really something rather special – because that's the way God made us.

You are a body...

God gave us our bodies. They are made up of chemicals which actually cost very little to buy. In fact, they are mostly water! But the body is put together in a complex and fascinating way.

Doctors have done a great deal in mapping out the workings of the body. They have tracked down causes – and produced cures – for a range of physical illnesses, even replacing some parts that wear out. But no one has ever actually created life except God. From birth to death, from conception to the last heart-beat, we live as a physical frame which is more finely engineered than anything we could ever make ourselves, and which, in the last analysis, is still a mystery.

Some religions and

... but you're more than just a body

philosophies say that our bodies are unnecessary – or even evil. They believe the physical side of life is unimportant. The sooner we can escape from our bodies, the better! But the Bible insists that our bodies are essential. It

says that we need bodies to be complete people. We're not always longing to escape from them into some pure 'spiritual' existence. Even the Christian view of heaven includes our bodies – rather different from our present ones, but still bodies.

The Bible does not teach that our bodies are evil in themselves. They're weak – and because we have some pretty powerful appetites, they can be a source of temptation, but there's nothing wrong with being physical. Jesus was!

Not all Christians in the past have realized this. They have taken something good like self-discipline to ridiculous lengths, giving the impression that physical activities such as eating and drinking, sex, or the bodily comforts and pleasures which make life easier to live, are somehow wrong. In certain circumstances we may be asked to give up any or all of these things if we're going to live for God, but under normal conditions they are as much part of God's design as breathing. It was he who gave us bodies in the first place.

Many people today would want to say that the body is all that we are.

But there is more to us than flesh and blood. The Bible also says that we are 'soul' or 'spirit'. These words have quite a range of meaning, but in their highest sense they signify the real you, the individual who thinks and feels, decides and does.

So many modern personal and social problems arise from the fact that we have forgotten that we are spiritual beings as well as physical ones. We also try to satisfy our spiritual needs physically and materially. The real you needs more than enough to eat and wear; it needs more than the things money can buy, because that's the way God made you.

Man or monkey?

The Bible teaching about people being something special was held by most people in the Western world until the nineteenth century when Charles Darwin's view about evolution began to become popular. Although his theory has been drastically modified since it first came out, his idea that all living things gradually developed from lower to higher forms of life **by chance** has been used to write off the Bible account of creation as old-fashioned and unscientific. Human beings, it is held, came from the same stock as the apes – even though the species parted company some millions of years back.

The same idea of inevitable progress was also applied to many spheres of life, for example, to religion, politics and to society in general. This belief made people at the beginning of the twentieth century very optimistic about the future, even though it meant coming to terms with the fact that we are really no more than higher animals. The history of the world this century – with its awful wars and suffering – has done a great deal to disillusion people and make them cynical about such theories of progress.

Although the view that we ascended from animals is widely held, we react very strongly when we are treated as animals – and we shout about our rights as human beings. We are appalled when people sink to what we call 'inhuman', 'bestial' or 'animal' behaviour. We might accept that we live and die like dogs in theory, but instinctively we know that there is more to it than that. The despair and hopelessness, the longing for purpose and meaning in life, the guilt, the doubts and the questionings of a generation brought up on evolutionary theory tell us that there has to be something more. No animal ever anguished over its existence as man does.

It is interesting to note that, apart from real difficulties with the original theory of evolution, a number of eminent scientists have questioned the whole idea. In their opinion, it doesn't account for all the evidence. So evolution is not the only **scientific** explanation of life on our planet. There are alternative theories.

Because the theory of evolution seems to be so very different from the Bible's account of creation (and the Bible's estimate of humanity), many Christians have dismissed evolution altogether. God made the world in stages, as in the Book of Genesis chapter one, with Adam and Eve, our first parents, coming into existence as a special creation which made them different from the rest. Others have argued that some form of evolution might well have been the method God used to get to this stage. Either way, Christians believe that God was in control of the process of creation, and that people are much more than animals.

Only one race

Every human being – no matter what their nationality, their sex, or the colour of their skin – is made in the image of God. This is the basis for what we call 'human rights'. There is a natural 'family of man', even though we often don't behave like brothers and sisters to each other. This means that the person eating in a New York restaurant is a brother to the beggar in Calcutta, trying to find enough food for that day. We are related and responsible to each other because of what we are.

The Bible clearly speaks out against racial discrimination, class distinction, economic oppression or anything which gives one person greater value than another. Christians believe that in spite of differences in colour, culture, class or status, we are all people, and equal in God's sight.

ESP and all that

Recently scientists have begun to take seriously something which is quite common, but which was laughed at or explained away for many years. We call it extra-sensory perception. It includes a number of different phenomena. There is telepathy, or thought transference; precognition, that is, knowing things before they happen; psycho-kinesis, the power of the mind to move or change physical objects. And there are the widely-reported 'out-of-the-body' experiences of those who have been medically 'dead' and then resuscitated.

It is certain that some of the 'evidence' given for these phenomena is either chance or fraud. But there is a great deal which simply cannot be explained by the normal rules of science, especially by those who say that humans are only a body. There's a sinister side to this as well. Some of these experiences have been exploited by those involved in occult practices – which are forbidden in the Bible.

However, what we know at present underlines the Bible truth that we are more than flesh and blood. We have dimensions to us that are more than just physical.

Solidarity

When the Polish free trade unionists chose 'Solidarity' as their title, they were using a word which applies to all of us. As human beings we are all inter-related and bound up together in the same bundle of living humanity. We live, we laugh, we struggle, we suffer, we hope, and we die **together**. This is what Paul in the New Testament meant when he spoke about the whole human race being 'in Adam'. It's in this solidarity that things happen to us which we can't help or avoid.

If you think that you're a solitary individual standing on your own, do a bit of arithmetic. You are the product of two parents. They were the product of four. Go back about ten or so generations and you are the result of over 4,000! What a mixture of genes we really are! We are really a product of the race as much as an individual.

This is important because the Bible tells us that God not only deals with us one by one; he deals with us together. What our parents do can affect us, just as what we do can affect others. Even what our first parents did had a far-reaching impact. The whole race was involved because of our solidarity with one another.

❝No man is an island, entire of itself; every man is a piece of the continent, a part of the main(land) . . . any man's death diminishes me, because I am involved in mankind; and therefore never send to know for whom the bell tolls: it tolls for thee.❞
John Donne

A BROKEN WORLD

What sort of creature can produce heart-stopping symphonies – and run death camps? What sort of mixed-up animal can build cities and engineer complex communications – and then threaten to blow everything – including himself – to kingdom come? What sort of mind can discuss, debate and philosophize while leaving half the world to go hungry?

Why is more money spent on killing than on healing? Why is more energy poured into destroying than into creating? Why is more effort expended on hurting than on helping?

People are born to poverty, live in fear, suffer without hope. They are herded, they are crushed; they are beaten, they starve; they are enslaved, they are homeless. And they die without anyone caring or even acknowledging they existed.

What's the answer? Doesn't God care? Where do we lay the blame?

❝O the grandeur and the littleness, the excellence and the corruption, the majesty and the meanness, of man.❞
Pascal

Something's wrong with the human race

Most people are agreed about that. There's such a gap between our lofty ideals, philosophies, aims and goals and what we actually achieve, that any realist just has to puzzle out an answer. And there have been a wide variety of answers to the puzzle:

'They can't help it. Its all part of their nature.'

Some people argue that the drives, urges and instincts with which people are born aren't their responsibility. We shouldn't be surprised if we see them behaving as they do.

'Man is born free and everywhere is in chains.'

French philosopher Rousseau blamed the mess on complicated society. It's all a matter of environment. Give people a nice, simple life-style, and their problems will disappear.

**'People are victims
of the economic system.'**

The Marxists blame the capitalistic
structure in which many live. Come the
communist revolution and people will be
liberated, free to be themselves.

'People don't know any better.'

Humanists believe ignorance is the
problem. Once people are shown that it
is much nicer to be kind and good to one
another than to be selfish and greedy,
then people will live in peace and
harmony.

**'It's part of human
evolutionary development.'**

Some people believe that the human problem is nothing more serious than growing pains. We are evolving from man to superman. What men and women need, therefore, is education and training if they are to realize their full potential.

> 'Everyone has sinned and is far away from God's saving presence.'

Christians believe that we were made for God, but that we have rebelled and gone our own way. The Bible calls this rebellion sin. And it says that by ourselves we cannot do anything about it. Only God can give us the help we need.

What me, a sinner?

Most of us are happy to talk about the fact that the world is in a mess – or to discuss the failings of the human race. But when we bring the problem closer to home, to what has gone wrong with me, we begin to feel very uncomfortable.

The Bible has a word for us: sinners. We regard that as a bit of an insult. After all, most of us do our best to live relatively decent lives. We're good to our friends, kind to kids, fond of animals. We get on as well as can be expected with our next-door neighbours. We don't break the law more than anyone else. So what's all this business about being sinners?

When the Bible talks of us as sinners, it is first of all talking about how we get on with **God**. This affects how we get on with others, but as we've seen, in the first place we were made for God. We may not steal or commit violent crimes – but do we love God with everything we've got? God is interested in the way we live our lives, and particularly in the place we give to him in our daily living. The greatest sin is not killing, stealing, or adultery. It's living day by day without a care or thought for God.

We can be quite religious and live like this! We can go to church, sing the hymns and all the rest, but if God doesn't have real control over us and what we do, we're as much a sinner as the person who never goes near a place of worship. **God doesn't want us to have a little 'religious area' in our lives. He longs to invade the whole of us – changing our lives from the inside.**

Everybody's doing it

In our better moments we all admit that we fall down in a whole variety of ways. We try to get out of it, of course. When we're put on the spot, we excuse ourselves and try to shift the blame, but in our heart of hearts we know that we're not what we ought to be by a long way.

This is why growing up is sometimes such a devastating experience. We have such high ideals when we're young about how people ought to behave, and it turns out to be very different from what we expect. We look out on the world scene with its dreary round of hypocritical words, its greed, its selfishness – and all the suffering and misery this brings – and we begin to get a little cynical. Then people we know well – our friends, and even our parents – begin to let us down. People we look up to fall off the pedestals we put them on, and we get disappointed and hurt.

But perhaps the hardest thing is to come to terms with the fact that when it comes to it, we can't live up to our own principles and ideals. With all our lame excuses, we modify them and come to terms with 'our little weaknesses' as we call them, settling down into the rut of moral failure. At this point many people give up and stop trying.

But for those who are morally serious this can be agony – which says something

Can't God stop the suffering?

Suffering in the world is a special problem for Christians because they believe in a loving God (who wants to stop suffering) who is also all-powerful (and therefore capable of stopping it). Yet the fact remains that suffering goes on, and God seems to do nothing about it. There are no simple answers to this problem, as anyone who has asked God 'why?' will know.

But Christians believe that the Bible, which is realistic about suffering, also gives us some pointers towards an answer.

● **The origin of suffering.** The Bible seems to lay the blame for a lot of the world's suffering at our doorstep. It says that God made men and women who could freely choose right and wrong themselves – and they chose to go against God. This has ultimately led to the modern problems of refugee camps, kidnappings and hostages, aggressive world powers, pollution, the nuclear threat, and so on. Making an enemy of God also makes us enemies of each other.

● **Why doesn't God stop disasters?** Couldn't God have stopped World War 2 happening or the Titanic sinking? The answer is that we don't fully know why God does not intervene in world events. But many Christians believe that it has something to do with the fact that God made us with free-will and does not want to rob us of it by stepping in whenever something is going wrong.

● **What about natural evil?** Why do earthquakes, volcanoes, floods and famines destroy valuable crops and wipe out whole communities? The Bible says that the whole creation has been spoiled by human rebellion against God. It even says that the creation is in chains – enslaved to decay and death. This situation can often be aggravated by human exploitation and misuse of the natural world.

● **God's involvement in our suffering.** Many people seem to feel that God is aloof from their suffering. But if the Bible is true we need to think again. Jesus, God's Son, suffered the rejection of his friends and an agonizing death partly to show us that God is involved in our pain – even to the point of experiencing it for himself. Jesus' resurrection from death shows his personal triumph over pain and death – and this is a triumph he has promised to share with those who believe in him.

A wounded Afghan guerilla is carried to safety after a bombing raid.

about what we are. No animal ever faced such crises of conscience, or spent so much time puzzling out the moral dilemma which faces every person ever born. The apostle Paul put it this way:

❝I don't do the good I want to do; instead, I do the evil that I do not want to do.❞ Paul

Why do we like sinning?

If we know what's right and good for us, why do we do the opposite? Why are we so self-destructive? Why don't we keep our own rules, let alone God's?

Is it just that we get into bad habits? It's certainly easier to do something a second time, or a third, or a fourth. The more we do what we know is wrong, the easier we feel about it. Conscience loses

its sharp edge. We gradually come to accept what might have once horrified us. We come to terms with our own failure.

But there's more to it than that. There is something in us, in our very natures, which *wants* to sin and which finds sinning attractive. The battle is not just with the Devil on the outside; the struggle also goes on inside. The Bible recognizes just that. It tells us that we are not just sinners because we have sinned; we sin because by nature we are sinners. Our sinful actions are just the outward signs of what we are inside.

❝It is what comes out of person that makes him unclean. For from the inside, from a person's heart, come the evil ideas which lead him to do

immoral things, to rob, kill, commit adultery, be greedy, and do all sorts of evil things; deceit, indecency, jealousy, slander, pride, and folly – all these evil things come from inside a person . . . **99**

Jesus

Just as a bowl with a bias built into it can never run anything but a curved track – it is always being pulled away from the straight – so we have a bias in our natures away from good and towards evil. For sinning is not just a matter of the things we do. It affects the way we think and feel; it distorts our attitudes and values; it has to do with our very natures.

66 How man fell I do not know; why men fall I know within myself. **99**

Kierkegaard

Family likeness

When we ask where we get our twisted natures from, we have to admit that we've had them as long as we can remember. Ask any school teacher, and they will tell us that 'sweet little children' can be selfish and cruel in the extreme. Even the smallest baby can be dreadfully demanding and self-willed, as many young parents have discovered. This is not something we have to learn. It's the good things we have to be taught; we do the other sort naturally.

All of which points to the conclusion that somehow, along with mother's blue eyes and father's curly hair, we inherit from our parents a much more sinister likeness. They share with us the sinful nature which dogs them through life, and with which they have had to struggle.

One of the Bible's themes is that everyone – no matter who they are – does wrong. From day one we have a bias to wrong passed on from parents to children.

The Bible does not spell this out in great detail. But many Christians believe that our sinful nature goes back ultimately to our first parents. In the creation story, Adam and Eve were given a moral choice, and they chose for themselves rather than for God. According to the apostle Paul, because our whole race is bound together in a special way, what they did affected all their descendants.

If a couple emigrate before their children are born, the children will grow up with all the privileges – or drawbacks – of living in their parents' adopted country. Our first parents emigrated to sin, and we are still living with the consequences.

❝Who is unhappy at not being king, except a deposed king?❞

Pascal

Bad as bad can be?

Does this mean that we couldn't get any worse? No, even we are shocked by the depths to which some people descend. In fact, in this respect we've been rather unfair to the animals. Our worst behaviour as human beings is not merely animal – it's worse than animal. Animals don't run to the extremes of torture that human beings do. They don't invent instruments of war, suffering and death. The author William Golding said that it is only humans who 'manufacture evil the way a bee makes honey'.

Having said this, it is true that the vast majority of people can live reasonable lives and get on with one another without too much friction. That's why they think they are really alright. But as far as God is concerned, we can't put a foot right. Whatever we might think we have achieved at a human level, if we leave

Caught in the act

The Bible writers used some shocking words to describe the mess we have got ourselves into.

● **Transgression** – breaking God's laws, disregarding the rules he laid down for human living. And as these are what he personally wants, this involves *rebellion*. Sinners are revolutionaries against God and his goodness.

● **Sin** – comes from the picture of an archer missing his target, with the arrow falling short of where it should have gone. We have fallen short of what we ought

to be as well as what we ought to do.

● **Iniquity** – means something that is twisted and out of true, like a piece of warped wood. Men and women are bent and perverted both in their characters and in their actions.

● **Uncleanness** – we dirty our hands when we sin. This word was also used to describe foul diseases for which there was no cure. Sinners are like sick people who need a doctor's help.

● **Debt** – we owe God our lives and everything

we are. When we misuse them, and when we declare our independence from him, we heap up a vast debt which we find impossible to repay.

What the Devil?

When analyzing their failures the Bible authors came to the conclusion that as well as trying to cope with their own evil tendencies they were also under pressure **from outside.** They laid the blame on a spiritual being they called, among other things, 'the Devil' or 'Satan'.

When God created everything, he made other spiritual beings besides men and women. We call them angels, and they move on and off the Bible scene quite regularly. Some of these, including one of their leaders, Satan, did what man himself did. They rebelled. They declared themselves independent and set up in opposition to God.

It was a hopeless sort of fling, of course. You can't take on God and get away with it. But until the great final reckoning, they have gone about causing havoc in God's world.

It's easy to be fooled about the Devil. He isn't the clown with horns and tail that he's often made out to be. He's a creature of high intelligence and real power who doesn't give an inch when it comes to bringing us down. It is Satan and his servants who tempt people to sin, who blind people to the truth, and who go out of their way to spoil God's work in the world.

But we can't blame Satan for our sinning. He has world-wide co-operation! We find temptation titillating, and sin enjoyable. We kid ourselves that God's laws were made to be broken. We ignore our consciences until we don't hear the warning bells ring any more. Although Satan has a lot to answer for, in the final analysis, when I sin I'm the one who gives in to his temptation – and usually because I want to.

Many people do not believe in the Devil. Others do, and get involved in his activities. Both of these extremes are dangerous.

him out of what we do, our whole lives are out of joint. We are off course and drifting. And even worse, we are lost and heading determinedly for destruction.

Guilty!

We all experience that part of us which we call conscience, which comes into play when we've done something we know we shouldn't. Ronald Biggs, the British train robber, was asked if crime paid. Although he was living in luxury on the proceeds of his crime, he disagreed. He explained that you couldn't alter what went on in your mind. It's never easy to live with a bad conscience.

But we mustn't confuse **feeling guilty** with **being guilty**. It's possible to suffer from a sense of false guilt sometimes when we haven't done anything wrong at all. We can feel bad simply because others – or even ourselves – have mistakenly convinced us that we ought not to be doing what we are doing.

But it's much more common to be guilty without knowing it. We can slip through life leaving God out of our calculations, and it's only when he shows us what we're doing that we see how far off beam we are. There's a moment of truth when we see things as he does, and when we realize what we're really like and where we're really going.

Sin not only involves us in chronic inability to be what we know we should be; it also leads on to judgement. This is because it involves breaking God's laws. Because God is just, then his judgement must follow sin as night follows day. There's no getting away with it as we might with human laws. God knows and sees everything, and one day he is going to call us to account for the way in which we have lived. For all our excuses, the judge on that day will pronounce the sentence of 'guilty' over every one of us.

The sentence that God must pass on sin is nothing less than death. This is not just physical death; the Bible describes it as being cut off from God. For death is separation. If we choose to live our lives shutting God out, then we mustn't be surprised if he shuts us out on the last day.

All these things are painful to believe – and they are painful to God, too. He did not make us in order to punish us, but so that we can enjoy life with him. Some people dislike the Bible because of its teaching on God's punishment of sin. But these ideas are written in the Bible because God loves us.

It's because God loves us that he tries to waken us to the real facts here and now. How can the doctor cure us if we don't face up to his diagnosis? How can God forgive us and show us what he can do with our lives if we don't admit that we're sinners? Jesus told us that he didn't come into the world for people who thought they were good enough; he came to rescue those who knew they were failures.

A noble ruin

The Christian estimate of where men and women are must be very different from those which assess human sinning and suffering as just a stage along the way to better things. In Bible terms, mankind is fallen. We are not what we were designed to be, and we live with a confusing awareness of that fact.

Human beings are like an old ruin. When we walk around the broken-down walls and look out through the empty windows, we can imagine what wonderful buildings they were **once**.

And if human theories about our condition don't measure up to the Bible's picture, nor do the human solutions which have been proposed. They're all doomed to failure, because only God can undo the devastation of sin and remake us in his original design. And that's what the good news of Jesus is all about.

5

THE MAN WHO WAS DIFFERENT

At the heart of the Christian faith there is a man. Not church buildings, creeds, rules and regulations, or even the Bible itself. Jesus Christ is not merely the founder of Christianity, but the person it is all about. Different people believe in different things, but almost everyone seems to be fascinated by Jesus. Even people who are hostile to the church find something strangely attractive about him. Who was he? What did he do and say that has earned him this unique place in history?

Three years that changed the world

Palestine in the first century AD was very much like a modern country under foreign occupation. There were foreign troops in the streets and local guerillas in the hills. There was forced labour and the occasional violent incident. Palestine was one small ingredient in the vast Roman Empire which then straddled the world. Roman rule was harsh, and the Roman peace an iron-handed affair.

The Jewish people smouldered on in

discontent, grumbling at the humiliation and high taxes, but unable to do anything about it. But then someone appeared among them who shifted the balance of power, not only for Palestine, but for the whole of history afterwards.

He was only in the public eye for about three years. He did what he did in a scrap of country about 125 miles (200 kilometres) long and 50 miles (80 kilometres) wide. His early life was lived in obscurity. His home and upbringing were peasant. He had little formal education. He worked with his hands.

As far as the authorities were concerned – both civil and religious – he was just a number, although inconvenient enough to have to be got rid of. So they put him down in the particularly thorough way they did in those days.

But what they thought was the end was, in fact, the beginning – of life, hope, light, joy, power, peace and so much more for millions unborn. For the Galilean peasant was no ordinary man. He was the Son of God.

The waiting game

Although crushed and humiliated, the first-century Jews in Palestine were not without hope. Part of their Old Testament faith was that they were God's special people. And God had pledged himself to step in and rescue them in times of trouble. He had done it in the past; he would do it again.

What is more, what they read led them to believe that it would be by means of a particular person. They had a number of ideas about who and what he would be like. Some expected another prophet like God's spokesmen in the past; others thought he would come as a High Priest like those who had headed up the nation a few years previously, though much more wonderful. But most people thought of him coming as a king.

It was some time since they'd had a king worthy of the name. They had to look back to Old Testament times to find anyone who came anywhere near the ideal. There King David had been

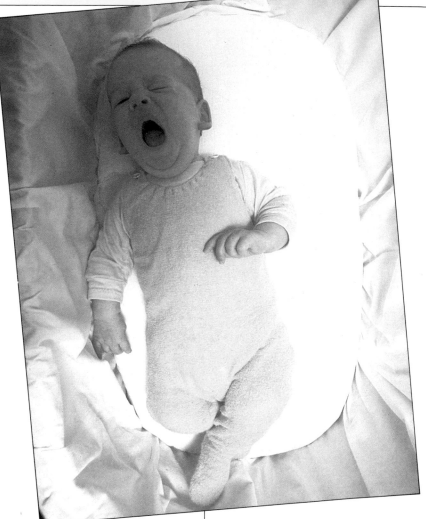

Every human birth is something special. But Jesus' birth was unique because as God's Son he had no human father. His mother, Mary, was a virgin when he was born.

singled out by God and, for all his faults, he had subdued Israel's enemies and established national prosperity and peace.

That was the kind of leader they longed for: a ruler who was also a fighter, someone who would throw out the Romans and set up a powerful, rich Jewish kingdom. Every time some rebel leader or other raised his banner against Roman rule the people's hopes came to life. But their hopes were dashed every time a revolt was put down. This was the sort of king they expected Jesus to be – and it's easy to see why they were disappointed. Because Jesus wasn't interested in a military kingdom, but in something far bigger. Something, in fact, which could include us today.

A touch of life

At the age of thirty Jesus left his home town of Nazareth and his job there as a carpenter and took to the road as a travelling preacher. This signalled the beginning of an extraordinary three years which were to mark indelibly the memories of those who saw and heard what went on.

There was something about Jesus which attracted people. They hung on his words. They listened, as they had listened to no other preacher or teacher, to what he had to say. His words were comforting, telling of a God who loved and who searched for sinners, and who forgave. His words were demanding. They called people to a higher level of commitment than they had ever known before, and set standards of behaviour which were humanly impossible. His words were hard, cutting through the hypocrisy of outward religion, showing people how serious it was to play about with God. His words were powerful. They stopped people in their tracks and diverted them into entirely different lifestyles.

And what Jesus said he demonstrated by what he did. Jesus could heal people who were sick – sometimes chronically sick, often incurably sick. He cooled fevers, made the lame walk, calmed the insane, made blind people see and deaf people hear, freed lepers from their awful disease – and even raised the dead.

No wonder people crowded to see him: the elderly, the poor, the ill, the depressed, the hopeless. Kids loved him. Crowds stood open-mouthed at the things he said and the miracles he performed. After Jesus had been through their village or town, nothing was the same again.

❝ I know men and I tell you that Jesus was no mere man. ❞

Napoleon

Messiah, God's chosen one

Messiah is just the Hebrew word for 'someone who is anointed'. It is the same as the Greek word 'Christ'. In the Old Testament, kings among others were anointed with oil when they were appointed. It singled that person out as the one God had selected for the job. By Jesus' time, Messiah was the title of the coming king.

Outside Palestine, among non-Jewish Christians, who did not share the Jewish hope for such a leader, the term 'Christ' began to lose its special meaning. It increasingly came to be used as we used it today, as part of Jesus' personal name. In a similar way, very early on in the history of the church, believers were nicknamed 'Christians', or followers of Christ.

But miracles don't happen . . .

. . . or do they? We can dismiss miracles only if we believe in a physical world governed by unchangeable laws of cause and effect. What happens today, it is argued, is what always has and what always will happen, whatever the circumstances. Miracles do not happen today – and therefore they did not then.

We might be able to understand Jesus' healings as a case of mind over matter, but people cannot walk on water or still storms – so Jesus could not either. We cannot change water into wine or feed thousands of people with a picnic lunch – so neither could he. Apart from resuscitation, the dead, once dead, remain dead – even for Jesus. So although he may have seemed to do these things – although his disciples may have wanted him to do them – they are actually impossible, and must be explained away.

But what about the God factor? If God really is involved in the daily running of the world, and if the laws of nature are his laws anyway, what's to stop him overriding them if he wants to? To say that God wouldn't do that sort of thing is beside the point, because the Bible, both in the Old and New Testaments, tells us that on occasion he did. What is more, the most outstanding demonstration is connected with Jesus' brief ministry. We may find this difficult to believe, but once we allow God into the equation, nothing is impossible.

The fact that Jesus had authority to do these things tells us something about him. They were one of the ways in which his Father singled him out as his Son while he was here on earth. People were faced with the evidence and left to draw their own conclusions.

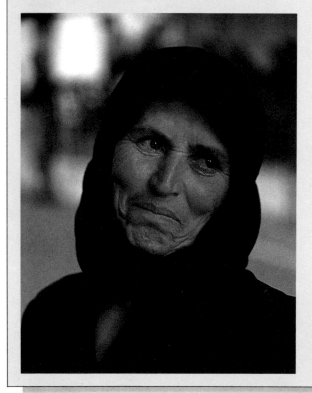

Perhaps the most remarkable of Jesus' miracles were his works of healing. Here he showed his deep concern for those who suffered.

The downtrodden and badly-treated have often looked to military leaders to solve their problems. Jesus came as his people's leader – but he refused to fit the military mould.

Jesus the storyteller

Although Jesus often taught his followers quite plainly and openly, he just as often spoke to the crowds in what are called 'parables'. Parables are stories with a spiritual meaning hidden away in them. He used the ordinary, everyday events with which they were familiar, and he did it in such a gripping way that his hearers were caught up in the action – and often surprised by the outcome.

Sometimes the point he was making was all too obvious. Sometimes only those who were in tune with him and his message realized what he was getting at. Sometimes even his disciples only understood what he had been saying after his death and resurrection.

What Jesus said about himself

In his teaching and in the demands he made, Jesus said some remarkable things about who he was and what he had come to do. It is true to say that no other religious teacher, in or out of the Bible, has described himself as Jesus did.

● Jesus forgave people their sins – something only God can do.
● He said he had come to fulfil God's Old Testament Law.
● He said he was the fulfilment of Old Testament prophecy as the Messiah, God's chosen one.
● Jesus described himself as God's Son, possessing a unique relationship with God as his Father.
● He said that only he could perfectly reveal God to men and women.
● He spoke of himself as the person who would one day judge the world in God's place.
● He asked for complete obedience on the part of his followers.

❝I am the way, the truth, and the life; no one goes to the Father except by me.❞

Jesus

Man of history

Some people have tried to argue that Jesus never existed as a historical person at all. This is the usual Marxist explanation of the story. But no reputable historian who has examined the New Testament evidence would take that position. It is usually those who want to prove a point or to underpin some philosophy of their own who argue in this way.

'It is not historians who propose "Christ-myth" theories.'
Professor F. F. Bruce

Real flesh and blood

Whatever else they might have had to come to terms with, Jesus' followers knew they were dealing with a man. He was not like one of the mythical gods of ancient Greece who were said to go on a spree by taking human form for a while. Nor was he, as some have suggested, an extra-terrestial being out of a flying saucer.

The Gospels tell us that he had a human body like ours, with all its functions and restrictions. He grew up, felt hunger and thirst, was tired and slept. He could suffer and bleed – he could feel, rejoice, grieve. At times he was angry; at others he was lonely. He spoke in a language they all understood, and he used ideas they were all familiar with. There were some things he did not

know, even though he knew a great deal more than anyone else.

Most significant, he was tempted as every man or women is tempted. The Bible tells us specifically that he was tempted to misuse his miraculous powers, to call attention to himself, to duck his Father's will for him. What was really different about Jesus was that he never gave in. He always was and did exactly what God his Father wanted.

In that respect he was what every human should be like, because sinning doesn't make us any more human – it makes us less. And Jesus was not less than a man – he was the only perfect man who ever lived.

Action and reaction

It was one of Jesus' closest friends, Peter, having seen what Jesus said and did, who finally went public with his conclusions about him: 'You are the Messiah, the Son of the living God.' For him, as for Jesus' other followers, 'Messiah' meant nothing less than Israel's military deliverer and future King.

But Jesus gave them all a shock. He admitted that he was the Messiah – but not the one they expected. Instead of driving out the Roman occupation troops, he would be betrayed to them and they would put him to death. And afterwards he would rise from death. Jesus' words were confusing and unwelcome. A dying Messiah had no place at all in their idea of things, even though it was common knowledge that what Jesus was saying and doing was proving an embarrassment to the Jewish authorities.

Because Palestine wasn't a very important place, the Jews were allowed a measure of freedom and self-government. The Jewish leaders, however, lived on a knife-edge most of the time. They hated the Romans, but they knew that if they weren't careful, they would lose what meagre privileges they had. So when the odd imposter arose, claiming to be a leader and raising a following, they bit their nails and hoped he would go away. In Jesus' case it was even worse for he was making what seemed to them to be crazy claims which added up to nothing less than blasphemy. You can't be reared to believe in no God but one and take happily to a man who speaks like God.

So to pre-empt trouble they bribed one of his followers. They arrested Jesus in a midnight swoop. They hastily tried him on trumped-up charges, and they handed him over to the Roman authorities as a dangerous agitator who was disturbing the peace. Pilate, the Roman governor, who was not known for his humane treatment of anybody, would have dismissed the case – but the Jews insisted and pressurized him into signing Jesus' death warrant. And as the Roman soldiers marched the stumbling figure out to the place of execution, the affair must have seemed as good as finished.

Mad, bad – or God?

Taking Jesus' life, miracles, and what he said about himself together (and the greatest miracle, the resurrection, was yet to come), we're forced to come to some conclusion about this unique historical figure.

Was he mad, making crazy statements, claiming in his own deluded way to be God? Shouldn't they have quietly shut him up for his own protection? No doubt that is what we would do to him today. But many people who reject the idea that Jesus was God agree that his general teaching is entirely sane. His teaching about God, love, faith, forgiveness, good and evil is streets ahead of anything else in the world's religious writings. What he said rings true to our own experience.

Was he bad? Was he an imposter who tried to manipulate people for his own gain or power? His lifestyle doesn't point to this. He lived as a peasant to the end. His possessions were minimal. He refused any political role. He called people to loving, giving and serving – and he lived that way himself. He knew the risks he was running, and he still did what he had to do. Humanly he had everything to lose and nothing at all to gain. And as for a character reference, even his enemies had to cook up charges to bring him down.

But that leaves us with only one alternative. He was what and who he said he was. He was nothing less than the Son of God – God with us for a brief time, sharing our limitations and woes, working for our healing and peace, and challenging us to live for God. People in his own time had to decide about him – and it's the same today. He was either who he said he was or we have to write him off as a deluded imposter, or a tragic martyr for a lost cause. We cannot remain neutral about Jesus.

JESUS IS ALIVE!

Death is a fact of life. The only future event of which we can be absolutely certain is that one day we will die. The certainty and the finality of death casts a shadow of fear across most people's lives. The Christian faith doesn't pretend that death is not a problem – and it doesn't ignore our fears. Christians believe that God has met and conquered these fears by allowing his Son, Jesus, to die, and then raising him back to life. It is this belief in Jesus' resurrection which is at the heart of Christianity.

❝ The first fact in the history of Christendom is a number of people who say that they had seen the Resurrection. ❞

C. S. Lewis

Did the resurrection really happen?

Christians believe that on the third day after his death and burial, Jesus rose from death. Was this a cleverly devised hoax on his part – or on the part of his followers? Or was it just their wishful thinking? What are the real facts of the case?

● **Jesus died and was buried.** The Romans were thorough in the treatment of their victims. Even after Jesus had died, they thrust a spear into his side to make doubly certain. His friends and enemies were all convinced that he was dead.

● **His grave was guarded and sealed.** The authorities were worried that Jesus' body might be stolen. So they had a large disk of stone rolled over the entrance to the tomb. It was so large that it needed more than one to shift it. They set a guard. If they were Roman soldiers, there would have been four, fully armed and under military discipline. For sleeping at one's post or deserting, the penalty was death. If they were Jewish Temple guards the penalty for sleeping on duty was a flogging. Stealing Jesus' body was out of the question.

● **The tomb was empty** – all the Gospels tell us this. John adds the peculiar eyewitness evidence that the grave clothes were still there, not scattered about as though they had been stripped off, but neatly folded as though the body had melted out of them. There is no evidence that they went to the wrong tomb. The same women who had seen Jesus buried on the Friday were the first ones to visit it on Sunday morning.

● **Jesus was seen alive after his death.** He appeared to individuals like Mary Magdalene, Peter and James – and to different groups on different occasions. These include a couple on the Emmaus Road, the inner circle of disciples, and more than 500 people at one time. The

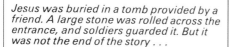

Jesus was buried in a tomb provided by a friend. A large stone was rolled across the entrance, and soldiers guarded it. But it was not the end of the story . . .

early preachers insisted on nothing less than the same sort of eyewitness evidence which is required in a court of law.

● **Jesus gave physical proof of his resurrection.** The risen Jesus was not a ghostly apparition – he was a living human being. He walked along the road with two disciples; he divided up the bread at supper; he invited his friends to handle him and see for themselves that he was real; he ate food with them; he challenged the doubting Thomas to put his fingers into the nail scars and his hand into his side as proof of his identity and of his resurrection. In Luke's account of

the resurrection, he uses the word 'proof' to describe the strongest type of legal evidence available.

● **What else could have changed the disciples?** The disciples were not expecting to see Jesus. Mary thought that he was a gardener, the others thought that he was a ghost. After his violent death they were scared and hiding. But only a few weeks after Jesus' death, they were confidently telling the crowds – and the very people who had arranged Jesus' death – that he was alive. Like Jesus, they had nothing to gain and everything to lose by doing this. The resurrection of Jesus had had an explosive impact on them. In their own words: 'We cannot stop speaking of what we ourselves have seen and heard.'

66 Do you believe because you see me? How happy are those who believe without seeing me! **99**

Jesus to doubting Thomas

God did it

Many of the New Testament quotes about Jesus' resurrection tell us that 'God raised Jesus from the dead'. The resurrection was the ultimate miracle in Jesus' career. This was more than resuscitation. God gave life to someone who had actually died, restoring him physically.

Anyone who does not believe in a God who can – and does – work miracles in this world, will have problems because of their starting point. They will think: 'Miracles don't happen; the resurrection was supposed to have been a miracle; therefore the resurrection did not happen.'

But to think like this is to come to a conclusion without giving the evidence a chance to speak for itself – without letting God be God. **If God is all-powerful, there is no earthly reason why he should not have done things this way if he chose to.** Our problem is often not with miracles but with the God who works them. To admit a miracle is to admit God – and that means that we must take him into account in our daily living.

❝ If Christ has not been raised from the dead, then we have nothing to preach, and you have nothing to believe. ❞
Paul

Where is Jesus now?

The Bible tells us that after his resurrection, Jesus appeared to his disciples over a forty-day period. During this time he explained to them why he had risen, and what he had come to do. Then, in an event known as the ascension, Jesus went off this earthly scene for the time being. He returned to his Father, sharing with him the control of human affairs and the destiny of the world.

One day, the wraps will be taken off, and everyone will see this for themselves when Jesus returns in splendour. Until that time he is working out his own plans on the earth by his Holy Spirit and through the church. It is in this way that he can be personally real to every Christian.

All you need to know about God

Jesus' disciples were not bashful when it came to talking about the message they had to share. For them it was the only message. Jesus was the only way to God, and the gospel was the truth about God.

They even went as far as saying that all truth, wherever you might find it, derives from Jesus as God's Son. They not only maintained that he stood behind the writing of the Old Testament, they were prepared to state that any insight, any true understanding anywhere came ultimately from him.

This was important in a world where men and women were looking for the truth about life, and it is just as important today. That truth, they said, was Jesus. So if someone is sincere in their search, they will recognize the truth of the New Testament message.

Solving history's riddle

Considering what small beginnings Christian teaching had, it made extravagant claims for itself. It not only proposed an answer to the ultimate questions of life and death, it maintained that it held the answer to the puzzle of where the history of the world was heading.

To the early believers, everything before Christ had prepared the way for him. In the Old Testament, God had specially set apart and educated his

Calling Jesus names

Jesus' followers were quick to draw their conclusions about the risen, exalted Jesus as we see from the letters of the New Testament. What they thought of him is often encapsulated in the names and titles that they gave him:
● **Christ** was a title which meant the Jewish Messiah, the long-promised King. By the time the good news of Jesus was preached to non-Jews, it became part of Jesus' personal name, and that is the way in which it is often used today. But the original Jewish meaning was that Jesus fulfilled in who he was and what he did all the Old Testament promises and predictions about a coming deliverer.
● **Saviour**, or 'deliverer'. God's Son had come into this world to rescue people from sin and its consequences in just the same way that emperors and generals had delivered whole peoples in the past.
● **Lord** was a word which could just mean 'sir', but which had also been used in the Old Testament as the Jews' special name for their God. In the New Testament, Jesus is seen as the Lord, ruling heaven and earth as a great king. Jesus was now the centre of faith for all Christian believers.
● **High Priest** was another Old Testament picture for someone who stood between God and people, helping them to be reconciled with God. Jesus now perfectly qualifies for this role of mediator, bringing people to God.
● **Son** was a name which Jesus used about himself. He often spoke about the close and intimate relationship that he had with God the Father. Christians also came to believe that God's Son had always been his Son – even before Jesus' life on earth.

people for the days when he would send his Son into the world. But also in the wider world, God had so worked that when Christ came, there was a spiritual hunger abroad which only the gospel could meet.

Equally, all history flows from the cross and the empty tomb as it flowed towards it. In the lives and experience of Christians, the powers of the new age are already at work. God is demonstrating to the whole world what he can do with unpromising material, changing sinners into people who reflect something of his own character, and in the process breaking down those age-old barriers of race, class, sex and status.

But the history of the world is not open-ended. The day will come when God's plan for the present time is complete, and when Jesus Christ will return as God's agent to wind up time and history, and to square accounts with men and women. Christians, therefore, not only look back to the momentous events of 2,000 years ago, they also look forward to that unspecified time when history will come to a conclusion. And the key to it all – is Christ!

❝I am the first and the last, the beginning and the end.❞
The risen Jesus

God become man

When we read the New Testament, there is no mistaking the fact that the early Christians thought that Jesus was much more than a man. His resurrection had convinced them of that. It was certainly true that he was fully human. One of the first errors about Christ was to say that he

What does Jesus' resurrection mean?

VICTORY!

The Bible sees the resurrection of Jesus as a great victory over all the evil forces at work in our world. Just when it seemed that Jesus had been completely defeated and humiliated by his enemies, he was raised from death in a glorious display of God's triumph. The great enemies of the human race – sin, death and the Devil – were put to flight. When Jesus returns to this world to wind up history, these enemies will be completely destroyed for ever. Jesus' resurrection gives us solid hope for the future.

DEATH DEFEATED

When Jesus was raised from death, it wasn't simply some private, personal experience that he went through. The Bible points back to Jesus' resurrection as the guarantee that God will similarly raise us from death in the future. If we are confident that God raised Jesus, we can be just as confident that he will raise to new life those of us who believe in him.

Because of this, Christians have a new attitude towards the experience of death. Death is not the end of us. Beyond it lies a much fuller life with God than we can imagine now.

This does not mean that Christians do not cry at funerals or that they take death lightly – death is still an enemy. But God has promised to rescue us from its clutches, and so we no longer need to fear it.

A STAMP OF APPROVAL

By raising Jesus, God placed a stamp of approval on Jesus' whole life and teaching. For the first disciples the resurrection was the piece of the jigsaw that held the whole puzzle together – it made sense of all that Jesus had said and done. It can help us in the same way. When we believe that Jesus rose from death, it helps us to come to terms with the things he said about himself, and to believe that he truly was God's Son, living among us.

JESUS IS ALIVE NOW

The resurrection isn't just something to read about in a book! Jesus is alive and can change our lives here and now. The Bible pictures him in heaven, reigning with God the Father. We can worship him, talk to him, bring him the problems we are facing. This is at the heart of being a Christian. When Christians think of Jesus they are not remembering a long-dead hero, but enjoying a close personal relationship with a living person. And as we allow Jesus to affect what we do and who we are, he gives us his strength to live in the way that we should.

wasn't human. Because of this, the early Christians insisted that he was just like us, although he never sinned, as we do.

But they did not stop there. Jesus had become the focus of their life and faith in a way that only God deserves to be. They worshipped him; they prayed to him; they sang his praises. When they spoke about Jesus, they frequently linked his name with that of the Father and the Spirit as together being the source of life, power and happiness.

On occasions they went even further. They described Jesus as 'always having the nature of God', or 'being the visible likeness of God', or 'being the exact likeness of God's own being'. Paul could write that 'the Son has in himself the full nature of God', and that 'the full content of divine nature lives in Christ, in his humanity'. John summed it all up when he began his Gospel:

66 Before the world was created, the Word already existed, and he was with God, and he was the same as God . . . and the Word became a human being and lived among us . . . 99

For the earliest Christians there can be no question about the fact that for them, Jesus Christ now had the same value as God himself.

In the following years there were many who disputed this, saying in a variety of different ways that Jesus was less than God – either as a mere man, or as some being greater than man but less than God. And so the church took steps to spell out what it actually believed about Jesus. They distilled the New Testament teaching into some simple, basic statements which have remained at the heart of true Christian belief ever since:

● **Jesus was really human** – though without the sinful nature which we inherit. Although he was tempted, he did not sin in any way.

● **Jesus was also God** – one with the Father and the Spirit. He came into this world by way of human birth, and yet as God's Son he has no beginning or end. As God he rightfully shares the worship and honour that we give to God as his creatures.

Who was Jesus?

In his own time, different people had different ideas about who Jesus was. Religious and social groups today also see Jesus in their own way:

● **Muslims** – Jesus was a prophet and special messenger from God to man. But Muhammad was *the* prophet.

● **Hindus** – Jesus was an incarnation of God, but one of many. He was not unique.

● **Humanists** – Jesus was a good man who taught high ethical ideals. His followers turned him into a god.

● **Jehovah's Witnesses** – Jesus was an exalted being, more than man but less than God.

● **Communists** – some believe that Jesus was a revolutionary, while others say he never existed at all.

● **Jews** – Jesus was a religious teacher who was not the Messiah.

Three into one won't go?

One of the most remarkable things about those who wrote about Jesus in such amazing terms was that they had been brought up to believe that there was only one God. All good Jews saw (and still see) this as fundamental to their faith. And the first Christians held this belief in one God to the end. However, something colossal had happened to them which made them speak about Jesus in the same way that they spoke about God – and to give him the obedience and worship they gave to God.

They also changed their views about the Holy Spirit. They already knew from the Old Testament that God's Spirit was divine – but now they began to speak of him as a person separate from both Jesus and the Father. Jesus himself had described him in this way, and it fitted in with what had happened to them when they had become Christians. **They had come to know God as their Father through his Son, Jesus Christ, by the personal power of the Holy Spirit!**

It was inevitable that sooner or later someone would read what they had written and start asking just how there could be one God when Father, Son and Spirit were all spoken of as being God. It took the Christian church some years to begin to talk about it, and even then they came little nearer to solving the actual problem involved. After all, when you're dealing with God, you're dealing with something you can never ultimately understand.

They finally put together what we know as the doctrine of the Trinity – that there is only one God, but that there are three persons, Father, Son and Holy Spirit. But this was not merely church teaching. The raw material for this belief lies in those amazing and perplexing statments about Jesus in the New Testament itself.

The ripples run on

Part of the evidence that Jesus' death was not the end is the fact of the church. From its remarkable beginnings when, in spite of opposition and persecution, the lives of many were completely changed, it has gone on to divert the whole course of world history. Adapting to a variety of situations and times, it has proved equal to all kinds of attempts to crush it. In fact, when Christians have been prepared to risk everything for Christ and even make light of death, they have attracted others by their buoyant faith.

Their achievements in society have been remarkable too. Because Jesus taught them to have compassion on those in need, they have been prepared to work and serve unselfishly to make this world a better place to live in. They have often been in the forefront of social reform, standing up for the rights of individuals and groups, defying attempts to erode the moral standards of society. They have been pioneers in the fields of medicine, education and social welfare.

And yet, Christianity is not a political movement as such. Christians even claim that their real home is beyond this world of time and sense, and that the greatest blessing they can share is faith in Christist. Their primary aim is to please him, not merely by their own efforts, but by depending on him for strength to do what they could never accomplish by themselves. For the Christian life is nothing less than direct contact with the resurrection life of Jesus himself, made real by the Holy Spirit.

In spite of many a dark chapter in their history when they have not lived up to what they have professed, that first little band of peasant believers has grown into an international fellowship whose influence cannot be ignored. In their own terms, Jesus Christ is the living Lord and reigning now – and that reign is expressed in hearts and lives given over to him and to his control today.

7

News extra:

Jewish rebel executed

Jerusalem, Good Friday, AD 29

ROMAN AUTHORITIES have today executed the popular preacher, Jesus of Nazareth, on charges of sedition and treason. In a few short hours, Jesus was arrested, tried by the Roman governor, crucified and hastily buried.

The authorities were aided by supergrass Judas Iscariot, and arrested Jesus in a midnight swoop on his Mount of Olives hideout. Charged at night – technically illegal, but reckoned to be necessary because of the pressing nature of the business – he was convicted by the Jewish Council of blasphemy on the evidence of several informers.

Apparently he had claimed to be God, and to be able to destroy and rebuild the Jerusalem Temple.

His case was referred to the Roman governor, Pontius Pilate, who alone can pass the death sentence. At first he refused to have anything to do with the case. But the angry mob that had gathered insisted that he was a troublemaker, and that he had claimed to be king of the Jews. During angry scenes, Pilate put the issue to the crowd to prevent a riot. They were given the choice of freeing either Jesus or the condemned murderer Barabbas. In a shock decision the crowd chose Barabbas. After the customary flogging, Jesus was taken out for crucifixion along with two thieves.

He was remarkably calm on the cross – unlike the crowd, terrified by a strange darkness which blotted out the sun from noon until 3 pm. At that time he died quietly long before the other victims. So end three years of mystery about this man who once delight the crowds, while disturb the authorities by his unauthorized activities.

WHY THE CROSS?

Death by crucifixion

Crucifixion was not a Jewish form of execution. In the time of Jesus, capital offenders were stoned to death – although sometimes the bodies of the executed were hung up for a day as a deterrent to others. This was infrequent as the Old Testament Law describes a person hanged by any method as somehow coming under God's curse. This may have been the reason why the authorities engineered Jesus' death at the hands of the Romans, rather than simply organizing a lynching (as later happened to Stephen, a disciple of Jesus). The curse of hanging would have been the end, so they thought, to any pretensions about Jesus being the Messiah.

The Romans used crucifixion as a method for dealing with condemned slaves, the lowest criminals, and particularly with political rebels in the provinces. As such it was quite common practice to crucify those who rose against Roman rule. We are told that when the Romans brutally put down a Jewish rebellion a few years after Jesus' death, they actually ran out of wood when dealing with the rebels in this way.

Roman citizens were never crucified. They were allowed the cleaner method of beheading. For the cultivated Roman, the cross was a symbol of horror and shame.

> **❝Even the mere word 'cross' must remain far, not only from the lips of the citizens of Rome, but also from their thoughts, their eyes, their ears.❞**
> Cicero

There were various types of cross. Some were a simple pole, others variations on two pieces of wood, the most common being either in the form of a 'T', or in the traditional shape as we have come to know it. Because Jesus' crime was pinned up over his head, it is most likely that his cross was this last type.

Traditionally, the condemned man would carry the cross beam – not the whole cross – to the place of execution. Jesus began in this way, but the soldiers very soon had to press a bystander into the job, which tells us something about Jesus' physical condition even before they crucified him. Jesus had been flogged and beaten up by the soldiers guarding him. He was crucified at a place called 'Golgotha' in Hebrew (meaning 'the skull') – a bleak hill outside Jerusalem where many criminals were executed.

The later followers of Jesus who wrote the New Testament did not overplay Jesus' physical sufferings, dreadful though they were. They believed Jesus went through something more than physical agony. He died to pay the penalty for the sins of the human race – and it was this suffering which became the central theme when the good news was preached. And it is for this reason that the cross, symbol of what is arguably one of the most horrific deaths by torture ever devised, became the symbol of the Christian message.

Visual aid

God's teaching methods were remarkably up-to-date. When he wanted to prepare his people for what was going to happen when Christ came, he used not only words, but also visual aids and drama. Both Jesus and his followers saw in the Old Testament system of priests and sacrifices a foreshadowing of the cross and of what took place there.

In the Old Testament, a priest's job was to represent the people and their needs (especially their sins) to God, while at the same time representing God to the people. The ritual surrounding them was elaborate, and it centred on the offering of sacrifices of various kinds.

The most important sacrifices involved animals which were killed and either offered entirely to God by being burnt, or eaten in part by the worshippers and the priests. An important part of the drama was the way in which the priests had to take the blood and use it in the ritual. We are told that the blood stood for the life of the animal, which was surrendered in death.

The lessons which God taught them through all this included the important fact that sin matters to God, and that the penalty for sin is death. If someone who has sinned wants to get right with God, that penalty must be paid in another way. This was emphasized by the way in which sins were often confessed over the animal's head before it was killed. The result of all this was 'atonement' (a word which means 'covering'). For people to be on good terms with God, their sins had to be covered, or put out of God's sight in some way. The climax of the year was the Day of Atonement when annually the sins of the whole nation were confessed and brought to God for covering.

The problem with the priestly scheme of sacrifices was that they could very easily become something done mechanically. This is exactly what happened in Israel's later history; People got into the habit of breaking God's laws – but thought they were alright because they kept up-to-date with their sacrificing. It was the prophets (people who spoke on God's behalf) who stressed the important side to getting right with God. People who sacrifice, they said, must be deeply sorry about their sins. They must be prepared to stop sinning, and to follow God's commandments. Without that, sacrifices – like any other kind of religious service – can become a sham and a mockery.

Ghastly mistake?

If Jesus' arrest and crucifixion took his followers entirely by surprise, it did not come as a shock to Jesus himself. On a number of occasions Jesus had predicted that he was not only going to die, but that it would be at the hands of the Romans. That could only mean one thing. Jesus knew he would be crucified.

The pattern of events told by Matthew, Mark, Luke and John reveals increasing opposition to Jesus and his teaching by the political and religious authorities as his fame spread. He was certainly safer in the north of the country away from Jerusalem, the centre of Jewish administration. Because of this, his friends were surprised and shocked when he insisted on making a journey there in order to celebrate the Passover festival – the high point of the Jewish year. When Peter had finally confessed that he believed that Jesus was the Messiah, Jesus had responded by foretelling his death, something which neither Peter nor the rest could stomach. Even more important is the fact that Jesus claimed that it would all happen as the Old Testament had predicted. His disciples, having read the Old Testament, expected a Messiah-King, but they did not expect his death in any shape or form. It was only after it had happened – and after the resurrection – that they were able to see that the cross was all part of God's plan for his Son, something which caused them to read the Old Testament again in a new light. Peter later expressed it in this way: 'Christ died for sins, once and for all, a good man on behalf of sinners, in order to lead you to God.'

For Jesus, death by crucifixion was no accident. It was the way in which God would meet our deepest need.

God in the dock

Because God is perfectly just, there was no way that he could simply let off those who had wilfully broken his laws. But because God is loving and merciful, he was deeply concerned about the fate of men and women, even though they would only be getting what they deserved. The cross shows us both God's love and his justice.

Jesus was fully a human being and so he could perfectly represent us before God. Because he was sinless, he did not deserve God's punishment. So he stood in our place in the dock, taking the sentence which we deserve. He paid the penalty for us, and on the cross suffered what we ought to suffer. Some Christians have even said that he went through our hell there. When he cried out, 'My God, my God, why did you abandon me?' something had come between him and his Father, and the only thing that separates a man from God is sin. He had no sins of his own; it was our sin that made him suffer as he did.

But Jesus was also God. So he was not only standing alongside the accused in the courtroom – he was also the judge. He was in absolute agreement about the sentence. What it all means is that in some way which we can't define, God absorbed into his own being – in the person of his Son – the wrath which was coming our way. God himself provided what God had demanded. His justice is satisfied; his love is fulfilled – and sinners who cannot help themselves have a way back to God.

Decisive battle

Part of our predicament is that the Devil has his way in this world of ours, exerting his evil influence over the lives of men and women. Sometimes he does this in violent ways, but most often his tactic is to make us apathetic towards God.

Against this enemy, Jesus came as a conquering invader. He attacked the Devil's kingdom frequently during his life, especially when he freed people whose lives had been satanically controlled. But on the cross he fought and won the decisive battle in his campaign, breaking the Devil's power, and stripping him and his forces of any authority they might have usurped for themselves. That's why what Jesus did is sometimes spoken about in terms of a

ransom or redemption – which means the freeing of a slave or a prisoner of war.

Satan may appear to be alive and well on planet earth, but he is a defeated foe. Because of this, Christians do not need to fear the Devil, although they may be severely tempted by him. It is only a matter of time before Jesus, like a general conducting mopping-up operations after a campaign, will have finally concluded the affair. Satan's days are numbered and he knows it – which is the reason why he will be making a last, final fling before Jesus returns. But the outcome will never really be in doubt, because the victory was won once for all on the cross.

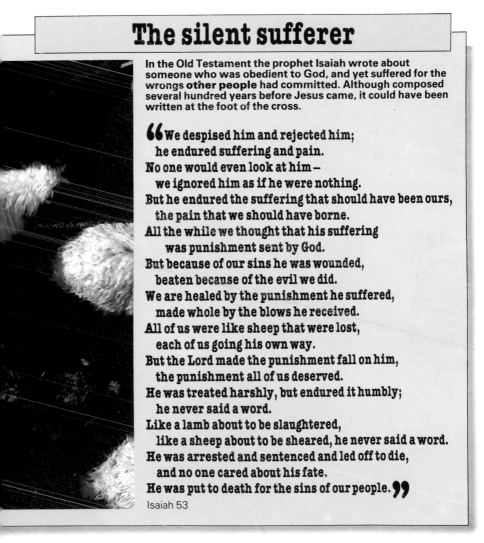

The silent sufferer

In the Old Testament the prophet Isaiah wrote about someone who was obedient to God, and yet suffered for the wrongs other people had committed. Although composed several hundred years before Jesus came, it could have been written at the foot of the cross.

❝We despised him and rejected him;
    he endured suffering and pain.
No one would even look at him –
    we ignored him as if he were nothing.
But he endured the suffering that should have been ours,
    the pain that we should have borne.
All the while we thought that his suffering
    was punishment sent by God.
But because of our sins he was wounded,
    beaten because of the evil we did.
We are healed by the punishment he suffered,
    made whole by the blows he received.
All of us were like sheep that were lost,
    each of us going his own way.
But the Lord made the punishment fall on him,
    the punishment all of us deserved.
He was treated harshly, but endured it humbly;
    he never said a word.
Like a lamb about to be slaughtered,
    like a sheep about to be sheared, he never said a word.
He was arrested and sentenced and led off to die,
    and no one cared about his fate.
He was put to death for the sins of our people.❞

Isaiah 53

Love finds a way

Martyrdom always exerts a pull. There is something about a man dying for a cause he believes in which makes us think that it must be worth dying for. But this isn't always true. Many people have died – even taken their own lives – horribly deluded and misled. Che Guevara dying in the Bolivian jungle, or bomb-throwing terrorists shot down on the streets of Northern Ireland do not make their policies any more sane. But the pull and the attraction is still there. Is that what attracts people to Christ?

Jesus was much more than a martyr. He knew exactly what he was doing when he set out on his last journey to Jerusalem – and it wasn't just to inspire pity on the part of potential followers. He went as the God-man to accomplish something only he could do.

Nor was the cross, as some people believe, just the supreme example of obedience and persistence that we must follow. It was an example, of course, and Jesus actually told would-be followers that they would have to take up their crosses if they were to follow him.

Because of this many Christians have been prepared to follow Jesus by going to their deaths. Archbishop Luwum was martyred in Uganda in 1977 because, as a Christian, he stood out against the evil policies of Idi Amin. And as Jesus prayed for his executioners, the Archbishop prayed for Amin when he was shot.

But the Christian life is not just a matter of gritted teeth in the line of duty. We need more than fine examples. We need the strength to copy them. We need outside help to overcome our sinfulness and free us from our sins.

Jesus was more than a martyr and his death was more than an example to follow. The cross shows us that God's love for us is so great that he was prepared to go to great extremes to rescue us from sin and death.

If I told my wife that, to prove my love for her, I would throw myself under a ᐧ train, she would have good reason to doubt my sanity. If, however, she had fallen in front of a train, and I threw myself down to get her out, that would demonstrate just how much I really loved her. Jesus did something like that. He threw himself into the path of the

The Lamb of God

'There is the Lamb of God, who takes away the sin of the world!'

This is how John the Baptist introduced Jesus to his own disciples. In other words, he was saying that Jesus was the one to whom the Old Testament sacrifices pointed.

In the Old Testament, a lamb chosen for sacrifice had to be a perfect specimen from the flock – not one that was just about to fall over and

die! As such it was a picture of Jesus' sinless life, lived out in full obedience to his Father. The blood shed in sacrifice was a picture of the violent death of Jesus on the cross in our place.

But there were several significant differences too. We do not have to provide our own sacrifice; God has done it. Jesus was God's Lamb. And he was no unwilling animal driven

to slaughter; he went to his death freely and willingly in love for us. In the Old Testament, there was no end to the sacrifices which had to be offered. They went on year after year, evidence that they did not really deal with sins. But Jesus died once for everybody, and that sacrifice has never had to be repeated.

oncoming judgement which we deserve perfectly well, because he loved us.

❝God has shown us how much he loves us – it was while we were still sinners that Christ died for us!❞
Paul

A personal faith

When the Son of God died on the cross, he made a way back to God for all men and women. **But that doesn't mean that the process is automatic. Each one of us has to realize that Jesus died for us personally.**

The death of Jesus is not just an event in history. Each person today has to decide how he or she will respond to his death.

But if anything is calculated to bring that home to us – to break our hearts, to make us grieve over our sins and wrongdoings, to turn us back to God – it is the cross. The fact that Jesus had to do that for me breaks down my defences and crushes my pride.

The fact that the Son of God – through whom the world was made – actually died in my place, taking what I deserve, makes me bow in adoring wonder. It is his amazing love for me which draws out my love for him, so that the obedience he demands is no chore, but a glad, willing response.

8

A NEW START

Excuses, Excuses

We all try to make excuses at some time or other – especially when someone tries to 'volunteer' us for something! We may have many doubts and fears about becoming a Christian. God knows our fears and doubts – and he cares about them. The Bible shows us how he can help us over these obstacles.

I could never keep it up.

'God, who began this good work in you, will carry it on until it is finished. . . ' The Christian life isn't just something you do or keep up. It's something God does in you.

I'm too bad to be a Christian.

'Christ Jesus came into the world to save sinners.' Which makes us all prime candidates. We are just the sort of people God wants to forgive and change.

Have you ever thought or said, 'If only I had my time over again . . .', or 'If only I hadn't taken that wrong turning . . .', or even 'If only I had known what I know now . . .'. For many people life is full of such regrets, but time, like an unstoppable conveyor belt, carries us on regardless. We know that we cannot simply erase the past – what's done is done and can't be changed. But is this right? The Bible seems to disagree. It tells us that there is a way to put the past behind us, and to make a new start in life – with God!

here's too much to give up.

esus said 'I have ome in order that ou might have life – fe in all its fullness.' eing a Christian isn't asy, and it may mean iving up some of the ings we like. But esus gives us a new uality of life now, nd hope for a future eyond death.

I'm doing quite well by myself.

'Everyone has sinned and is far away from God's saving presence.' That's his estimate of how we're doing. None of us can really do without God.

I'd rather put it off till later.

'Listen! This is the hour to receive God's favour; today is the day to be saved!' Later may be too late. Following Jesus isn't like an unpleasant duty to put off for as long as possible. We can experience God's love in our lives now.

Behind bars

Starting again with God usually begins, curiously enough, not with a sense of God, but with a sense of need. The first thing God's Holy Spirit shows us is that there's something missing in our lives. He does this to sharpen our appetites for the things that really matter. We don't want to eat until we first feel hungry, and the Holy Spirit makes us hungry for God.

It happens in a thousand and one different ways. It might be that despite all our achievements and fulfilled ambitions, we still feel that we haven't arrived as we thought we would. Or it might be through personal suffering and loss as our world falls apart at the seams. Many people need to feel some disappointment with life or themselves before they can admit that they need God.

Added to this, for many there's a feeling of littleness and insignificance in a big and brutal universe. They feel like ants running around in the path of a road roller. Nothing they can do or say or think has any impression on the mad, mad world around them. Often (though secretly) they're afraid of life and living.

And more than afraid, because tied in with all this for many of us is the unwelcome fact that we have failed. Whatever ideals we had have either been ditched or seriously modified in the rough and tumble of everyday life. And in their place there's a nagging sense of guilt. We know we're not what we ought to be – not even what we want to be – but there seems to be no way out.

And that's exactly where the Holy Spirit wants to bring us to. As long as we feel alright, that we're making it ourselves, that we don't need God to interfere in our lives, we will never realize all that Jesus Christ can do for us. But when we hit the bottom and honestly confess our spiritual bankruptcy – that we can't live this life without help – then God can do something. The Holy Spirit actually puts us behind the bars of our own anxiety, fear and guilt – so that he can let us out and set us free!

❝People who are well do not need a doctor, but only those who are sick.❞ Jesus

Acquitted!

The trouble with our questioning and searching is that too often we look in the wrong places and ask the wrong questions: 'What am I here for?' 'How can I be happy and fulfilled in life?' 'How can I attain my ambitions?' These may seem to be the right sort of things to ask, but they miss the real issue like arrows that fly off the target.

The real problem is put quite simply. God made us for himself. Like everyone, we have sinned, and our sin has cut us off from God. We need to get right with God and to live for him.

At the heart of the problem lies our sin. We have gone our own way. We have lived without God. Because of this we are guilty before God, cut off from him like friends who have quarrelled. And there's nothing we can do about it ourselves.

And this is where Jesus comes in because, as we've seen, he was not only perfectly qualified to represent us as an advocate speaking on our behalf, he actually died in our place, taking the penalty we deserve. That's why, although we stand in the dock guilty and condemned, the punishment has been taken by someone else – and we can go free! This is forgiveness – and more than forgiveness. God is prepared to acquit us, and regard us as innocent people, even though we've made an utter mess of our lives. He's ready to give us a new start in life.

When that happens we get right with God, and everything else begins to fall into place. It's like putting a dislocated limb back in its socket and knowing the sheer relief of having joints and muscles working properly again because that knee or shoulder is where it should be.

We begin to see why we're alive and what we're living for. We begin to get things into God's perspective, and the bigness of a threatening world takes on its proper proportions. We begin to know just how much God loves us, and our love affair with him spills over into all our relationships with other people. Life is worth living because we know Jesus Christ.

66 When anyone is joined to Christ, he is a new being; the old is gone, the new has come. All this is done by God, who through Christ changed us from enemies into his friends and gave us the task of making others his friends also. **99**
Paul

It's free – but it isn't cheap

There is nothing – absolutely nothing – that we can do to earn or buy or deserve the new life God wants for us. Many people try to please God – but under their own steam. In a wicked world, they attempt to keep their morals intact. In an irreligious world, they spend time, energy and money on services, prayers and rituals in the hope that God will see and accept them. The Bible tells us that these things are all good, but they do not mend our broken relationship with God. Only God himself can do that.

God has to do it all for us – and he has done. Christians talk about God's grace, which means his love for the undeserving which can never be bought or bargained for in any human deal. We have to accept it like a vastly expensive present which we could never, ever pay for.

But although God's love is free, it isn't cheap. Jesus was the one who paid the tremendous price of our new life with God. The price he paid was his own suffering and death.

About turn!

Becoming a Christian involves many changes in our lives. As God makes us his friends, the first change we notice is a change of heart about him, and about our way of living. We begin to want to do the things that please him. It means facing up to the fact that sin is sin – and turning from it. The Bible calls this inner change 'repentance'. But it isn't just an inner change. Repentance isn't just being sorry for our failures. Real sorrow for sin leads us to break with our sins, to turn our backs on them.

Unfortunately we've been reared in a 'can't help it' generation. We've been told that what we are is the result of our genes and our circumstances, and that we can't change. But God can change us. If we mean business with him, he gives us the grace and the strength not only to face up to our failures, but also to finish with the things he hates.

God will start to show us where our lives need changing. He may put his finger on one particular sin which has dogged us for a long time. It might be

Brand new life

Becoming a Christian is not just turning over a new leaf or brushing up an old life. It's an absolutely new experience, and the New Testament authors never tire of telling us that.

● **New birth.** Jesus spoke about becoming a Christian as 'new birth' We start life all over again. But God, like a good parent, doesn't abandon us. He gives us strength for this new life. Think of the potential wrapped up in that little bundle we call a baby – potential for living and growing, for breathing, feeding, moving, for

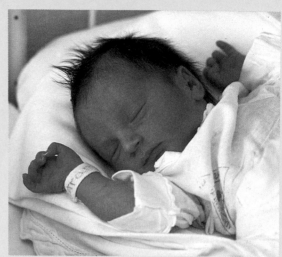

feeling, thinking and loving. Everything that makes up living is already there. God gives us all that we need for the Christian life.

● **New creation.** God called all the detail and the beauty, all the power and resources, and the rich variety of creation into being. And he does the same sort of thing for us. The person who sent the stars on their way and put the moon in orbit – the person who built the mystery of atomic structures into the fine detail of the universe – is the one who now takes our lives in hand. He remakes, reshapes, rebuilds, recreates. He takes the original designs he had for us, and turns us into the kind of people he always had planned.

● **New life.** God raised Jesus from the dead, and so, too, he gives us new life. The same resurrection power comes to bear on us. We were cut off from God because of our sins. The Bible takes this situation so seriously that it describes us as being 'dead'. The Holy Spirit breathes spiritual life, health and energy into our personalities, giving us a quality of living we never knew before. In fact, we find that we've never really lived at all until we meet Jesus.

All this means that Christian living is something which only God can do for us and in us. It's nothing less than a miracle which can change ordinary, drab, purposeless human lives beyond all recognition.

our explosive temper. It could be mistreating people who work for us, or fiddling our tax return or our time sheets. It might be an illicit relationship, or neglecting our partners and children. This is where we begin. It's not where we will end, because a life lived for years without God is going to take some sorting out. But as God spotlights the wrong areas in our lives, he also gives us the strength and the desire to put them right.

❝To do so no more is the truest repentance.❞

Martin Luther

Give in to God

Becoming a Christian means to give your life to Jesus. If he is going to do what he wants to do with you, he must have everything, no holds barred. Jesus is Lord – that means he's the boss now, and that your life is under new management. That's the heart of what is meant by faith.

Faith is a rather elastic word which can stand for things other than real trust in Jesus. Some people will say that they are okay 'because I have my beliefs'. But **what** we believe in is even more important than belief. It's important that we start to believe in Jesus. Other people are quite happy to say that they believe in God and in Christ, but they are not prepared to act on it. It stays in their heads. They believe **about** Jesus rather than trusting in him. The Bible hints that even the Devil believes in this way!

Real Christian believing involves nothing less than wholehearted commitment to Jesus. It involves loving him and obeying him. It involves putting him first in our lives before anything and everything else.

Take the plunge!

Learning how to swim is all a question of trust. You have to learn that the water will hold you up and not let you down. You might watch others swimming around, thoroughly enjoying themselves – but you're not doing it yourself. Nothing will happen until the day you get into the water and launch out. Everyone has to prove swimming for themselves.

If you're still teetering on the edge of faith, wondering whether or not Christ will do what he's promised, those of us already afloat can only say one thing : 'Come on in! It's marvellous!'

Born again

Becoming a Christian is such a radical change that Jesus said it was like being born all over again! And like childbirth, starting the Christian life is a unique experience for every individual. For some people this experience might have happened in a church service, or as they were quietly praying in their room, or as they were faced with some overwhelming crisis in life. However it happened, it was a deliberate (and sometimes a dramatic) experience which turned the whole of life inside out. Other people don't have a single experience they can look back on. They have gradually become more aware of God in their lives.

A baby only fully begins its human life on the day it comes into the world. But that birth was only the end result of a wonderful process of human development and growth which began nine months before. In a similar way, God is at work in our lives long before we know it, and even those who come to a crisis decision can often look back and see the process which led them to that step. God deals with us as individuals. With some people he takes longer than others. With some people he has to be more pointed than with others. Some babies take longer to be born than others!

The question we need to ask ourselves is, 'Do I really and sincerely trust in Jesus for myself **now?**' Because in the end, being a Christian is not just a case of making one decision, but of deciding every day to trust God with our lives.

When there's life around, sooner or later you notice it. When a new-born baby comes into the world, it wastes no time in telling you that it's alive! When a seed has germinated it breaks up through the soil into bud and flower. The new life that God gives us when we trust in Christ shows. In fact other people are often more aware of it than the person concerned – just as the proud parents are more conscious of their healthy new baby than he is himself.

❝The Church is a house with a hundred gates; and no two men enter at exactly the same angle.❞
G. K. Chesterton

Signs of life

We begin to want different things. God gives us a whole new set of appetites, so that we actually *enjoy* Christian things, even though we previously may have had no time for them. We want to be with other Christians. We want to worship God. We want to learn more by reading the Bible and going to church. It becomes natural for us to pray about the details of our lives. We want to share our new-found faith. We're ready to stand up and be counted, even though it might cost us our popularity and friends. We can say, quite sincerely and simply, that we now love Jesus Christ who first loved us, and that we want to follow him more than anything else in the world.

We begin to understand God's truth. The Bible begins to make sense. What Jesus did, and who he is, becomes real and important for us, even though we might have first heard about him years before. We begin to see how God can speak to us through the Bible today. One of the perplexing things however, is that although it all seems so simple and straightforward to us, our old non-Christian friends, and sometimes even our own families, don't seem to understand the good news about Jesus at all.

We begin to live in a new way. We used to live for Number One – doing what we wanted. But now we begin to ask what Jesus wants us to do, and what pleases him. We also come to see that there are some things which we have been doing which he must positively hate, and which must go if we're to live for him. But we're not on our own, because he not only helps us to break with our sins, he gives us the strength to live the kind of lives he has called us to live. Others begin to see a new kindness and honesty and decency about us, for this is the beginning of a whole new lifestyle.

9

TAPPING THE POWER

Imagine the frustration of having the very latest colour television and video tape recorder – on a desert island where there's no electricity. And electric gadgets are useless in your own home if there's a power cut or if they're not plugged in. It can be just as frustrating trying to force ourselves to live by God's rules, without the power to do it. When it comes to Christian living, there's no question about the power being available. After all, we're dealing with God, the greatest power source of all. But we're not going to get very far, or do very much that's useful, unless we're tapping that power in our lives. We need to be plugged in.

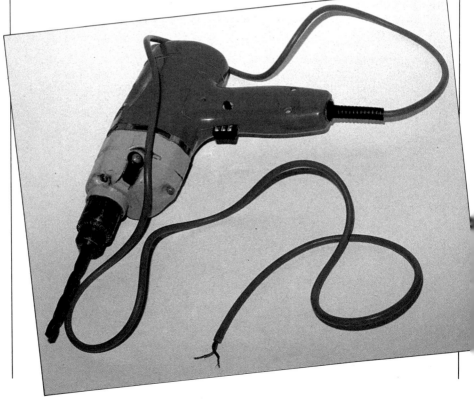

Danger! God at work

When Jesus came, he fulfilled all the Old Testament predictions about the coming King, including the fact that he was given power by God's Holy Spirit for his work on earth. But when Jesus got ready to leave his friends, he began to speak about the Spirit in a new and unexpected way. He taught them that the Spirit was not just a force but a person, who would come to the disciples after Jesus had returned to his Father. As a man, Jesus could only be in one place at a time. But the Spirit could be everywhere, because he would take up residence in the heart and life of each believer.

Jesus spoke about the Spirit as God at work, active in his world. He shows people their sins. He helps people know Jesus as a real person. He teaches us all that we need to know about Christian living. But above all, he gives us the power we desperately need to do the job Jesus has given us.

This power operates in two ways:
● It extends what Jesus did in his life. The Holy Spirit helps us to speak and act for Jesus in a Godless world.
● It is power for living the kind of life that pleases God. In his teaching, Jesus set us standards which are humanly impossible. But he also promised to give us the power we need to put these things into practice. It is at this point that the Christian message is different from any other kind of religion or philosophy.

❝I will give you a new heart and a new mind. I will take away your stubborn heart of stone and give you an obedient heart. I will put my spirit in you, and I will see to it that you follow my laws and keep all the commands I have given you.❞
God's promise in Ezekiel

This desirable residence . . .

When someone becomes a Christian, Jesus moves into that person's life by the Holy Spirit, rather like an owner-occupier moving into a house. And like every home-buyer, he then proceeds to turn that house into his own home. The rubbish is thrown out. The decay and damage are put right. The place is redecorated. Sometimes new bits are added. New furniture is moved in so that in the end the former owners wouldn't know the place.

When Jesus moves into our lives he begins a similar sort out. The accumulated junk of years – old ideas and motives, old ambitions and standards – have to go. He begins to deal with those psychological weaknesses and hangups which we'd resigned ourselves to. He breaks the stranglehold of habits and sins which we could never do anything about ourselves. And in their place he brings new desires, new appetites, a new will to live for him and to please him in what we do.

It's essentially a change on the inside. What happens on the outside, in terms of what we do or don't do, follows automatically. Christian living is the result of having Christ living inside.

❝It is no longer I who live, but it is Christ who lives in me.❞
Paul

❝Every time we say 'I believe in the Holy Spirit', we mean that we believe there is a living God able and willing to enter human personality and change it.❞
J. B. Phillips

Wind of the Spirit

Throughout the Bible, God enabled people to do what they couldn't do naturally by themselves. When he wanted a wise leader or a powerful spokesman or an effective general, he gave the people he chose to do the job special abilities which they did not possess before. And he did it by his Holy Spirit.

The Hebrew word for 'spirit' also means 'wind' – and God frequently stirred up a hurricane in the lives of people in the Old Testament. Shy, blushing types were turned into bold, brave men and women of God. Tongue-tied, stammering failures became powerful, eloquent leaders who performed feats beyond their wildest dreams – or nightmares.

However, only a few people experienced the Spirit like this. They were prophets or national leaders – and it was sometimes a temporary arrangement. God might withdraw his gifts if they sinned – which they often did. Although they had God's special strength to do their particular jobs, their own personal lives were far from perfect. It was as though they needed more than this.

The prophets were the ones who pointed forward to the future. The days would come, they said, when a Spirit-filled King would appear among them, and God would give his Spirit to all his people, even those with the lowliest jobs. This was great news – but there was even more in store.

The real problem with the Old Testament arrangement was that the people had God's Law (they knew what was right) but they didn't have the power to keep it. As we all too often discover for ourselves, knowing what is right is not enough. Human nature is so twisted that knowing the rules often tempts us to break them!

The problem lies in our hearts, and that's what God must change if we are ever to live lives which please him. The prophets of the Old Testament foresaw this, even if they did not experience it themselves. This was to be the basis of what was called the 'New Testament' – a new agreement between God and mankind, which would come into being when the promised King came. By his Spirit, one day, God would write his Law on their hearts. He would not only forgive them their sins, he would give them what they needed to stop sinning and to start living for him.

Metamorphosis

Caterpillar to butterfly; sinner to saint. It's the same kind of process. If we co-operate, God is prepared to transform and change us from the grovelling things we were into the things of beauty that he wants us to be.

The end he has in mind is nothing less than remaking us in the original design, like himself. And because Jesus was everything a human being should be, it means becoming like him in our character and behaviour. We begin to think like Jesus. We start to share his concerns. We learn to love like him, serve like him, and act like him. The Holy Spirit is the person who brings about this change in us.

Some people might think this is a bit scaring – that we get taken over and disappear as individuals. But we need not be frightened. Jesus wants us to be ourselves. We are never more human, never more ourselves, than when we're living out the potential of Christian experience.

The change that Jesus wants to bring will take time – a lifetime, in fact. Although we have everything we could ever need for living the Christian life in the Holy Spirit, we're such tangled, mixed up people, that it takes years for God to unscramble us and remake us.

But the target is always there before us, even though the job will only be completed when we finally see Jesus face to face.

There may be some gigantic steps along the way when we overcome some weakness in our lives, or when we launch out with God in new dimensions of obeying and trusting him. He has so much for us that he thrills and fills us with his Spirit in a variety of ways as we proceed. **But the most experienced Christians have always said that when it** comes to proving everything God could do for them, they could never say that they had finally arrived. However far we may have gone, with God there's always more.

Flight plan

No commercial airline pilot ever takes off not knowing where he's going, or merely makes up his mind as he goes along. There's a set destination and a flight plan which is worked out beforehand. His job is to keep the plane on course, picking up the beacons, looking for the lights, following his radar and doing what he's told from the control tower.

Nor is the Christian life a haphazard, chance affair which is left to us to work out as we like. One of the greatest discoveries a Christian can ever make is that God has a plan for our lives. Of course, his overall purpose is to change us into his own family likeness. But he's also in control of the circumstances of every day. He's got a job for us to do, people he wants us to meet, opportunities for us to take. Our job is to stay on course.

We do this by keeping in touch with control. That's why prayer is so important for a Christian, and why

God's choice – or mine?

When we become Christians, we face up to facts about ourselves, we turn from our sins, and we trust in Christ. God lets us in on his tremendous offer of forgiveness and life, and we take it for ourselves. It isn't always that way, of course, because some people react otherwise. They hate God for telling them the truth about their sins; they refuse to listen to the good news; they turn their backs on God's gift. So becoming a Christian is my choice. I have to exert my will, and if I turn down what is the only way out of the mess I'm in, I have only myself to answer for the consequences.

And yet the Bible tells us that's not the whole story. Long before we begin to think of God, he is at work in us. Our very unrest and dissatisfaction with life are prompted by the Holy Spirit in order to turn us to Jesus for relief. And much more than this, for the Bible teaches that those who believe were actually in God's mind before time began. They chose God, but more importantly, he chose them. They discover that it was part of his plan that they should be in that place at that time hearing about the gospel. They begin to realize that it was God who turned them to himself, giving them the power to choose rightly.

Whole books have been written on where God's will and ours meet – without solving the problem. We have to admit that, in the final analysis, it's a mystery – the same sort of mystery involved in being born. Long before the actual birth, the child is being formed in the womb.

And what is that bright little personality – that new individual – which comes into the world? Is it just a human product, the result of the chance of sex? Or is there more to it than that? In a similar way we may never know until we get to heaven where the human and divine sides of Christian experience meet. What we do know, however, is that it isn't just a matter of human effort and endeavour. God had a vested interest in us before we ever turned to him – and that's a great assurance.

reading the Bible for ourselves is part of daily living. In ways like these we get in step with God's mind and will. And because he is God, we also know that nothing can come our way which he hasn't allowed and which he will not give us the strength to cope with. In fact, we can even accept sufferings, losses and the reverses of life because we are sure that he knows best. Like a pilot flying blind who has to trust his instruments, we can have confidence in a Father God who works out everything in his own time.

Through the fire

Although being a Christian is a wonderful and exciting life to live, it doesn't mean that the sky is always blue and the sun always shining. On the contrary, Christians not only get their share of this world's troubles and suffering, but they also run the risk of getting more than their fair share! The Christian faith is no guarantee against suffering.

In a sense, becoming a Christian is asking for trouble. By taking sides with Jesus, we gain a bitter enemy, the Devil, who is out to seize every opportunity to bring us down if he can. He tempts us to do evil, and stirs up opposition in the world. Other people begin to resent someone who lives for God. And so they may well make life unpleasant for Christians, and in some situations that means actual physical suffering, and even death.

When these kind of things come our way, how should we react?

● **The Christian hope lies outside our world** – along with its pleasures and pains. We can look forward to the future when the work God has begun in us will be complete. This doesn't mean that we opt out of this life. God means us to live fully in the here and now. But ultimately

Temptation

Becoming a Christian is like becoming a new person. But the 'old us' doesn't give up the struggle easily. That's why a Christian can still sin, and that's why overcoming temptation is often a fight. It's like a tug of war going on inside. Our old habits and desires start to fight against our new loyalty to Jesus. So how can Christians cope with temptation? It helps us to know how temptation works, and how Jesus faced it:

● **Temptation isn't sinning.** We needn't feel guilty just because we're tempted – after all Jesus too went through temptation. It's only when we give in that temptation becomes sin.

● **Temptation is tailor-made.** We are presented with temptations that fit our own particular weaknesses. For some people it will be their pride, for others hoarding wealth, for others criticizing people. We need to know our own weaknesses and be honest about them with God.

● **Temptation is a clever mixture of good and evil.** Not many of us are tempted to do the completely evil things – like cold-blooded murder. With most of our temptations we are able to persuade ourselves that 'they aren't really that bad'. But this mixture of good and evil is explosive and can badly injure us.

● **Temptation gets us to doubt God.** Our temptations often insinuate that God is really an old miser who wants to stop us enjoying ourselves. Only by sinning can we get the things we need. This is the Devil's real aim in tempting us. He wants to come between us and God. We need to see temptation for what it really is.

● **Temptation's weak point.** We can fight back against temptation by hitting its weakest point. When Jesus was tempted, he used the Bible to resist the Devil. This doesn't mean the Bible is a magic book that will drive back the Devil, but that by knowing it inside out and living its message for ourselves, we will grow strong in doing good and resisting evil.

● **Temptation has been defeated.** Jesus was tempted but he did not sin. This means that he knows how we feel

we look beyond this life for our hope.

● **The symbol of our faith is a cross**, a symbol of suffering. Jesus told his followers that they should expect similar treatment if they were to follow him. So we share in Christ's sufferings. This also means that we can take our pains and sorrows to God, who fully understands how we feel. He too knows what it is to suffer.

● **Sufferings of various kinds are described in the Bible as a melting pot used to refine gold.** As the temperature rises, all the impurities separate out from the precious metal, and the result is pure, refined gold. God often uses our sufferings – if we're prepared to let him – to refine and purify our Christian lives, strengthening, not weakening, our hold on him and on his promises.

● **The way Christians suffer can also have an effect on other people.** The best many people can make of this troubled world is to put a brave face on things, and stoically resign themselves to whatever comes their way. But Christians believe that God the Father is in control. If we suffer, it is not through blind fate, but because God has called us to go through it. And God will also give us the grace to bear our suffering and turn it into something good.

when we are tempted – he understands and sympathizes with us. But he does more. He offers us real help, because he overcame sin. We can rely on him to help us in trouble. And when we do sin, he will pick us up and give us the strength to fight again.

❝You can't stop the birds flying overhead, but you can stop them nesting in your hair.❞
Martin Luther

In the early days of the church, when Christians were being tortured and executed for their faith, the way in which they were prepared to suffer attracted many people to Christ. One early Christian writer, Tertullian, said, 'The blood of the martyrs is the seed of the church.' Even if we aren't called to suffer quite like that, as the ordinary Christian copes with the sufferings and struggles of life with God, others see the difference.

❝It's unnatural for Christianity to be popular.❞
Billy Graham

On to the finishing line

If I have become a Christian, can I go back and become unconverted again? If I've started to run the Christian race, can I drop out and give up? If I've been saved, am I always saved, or can I be lost again?

After all, there's a great deal in the Bible about continuing once you've started. That picture of the Christian life as a race is one of the favourites. It reminds us that we've got to co-operate with God. We need to get up and get going. Just as the athlete grimly drives himself forward over the marathon miles,

How can I be sure?

How can I be sure that I am a Christian? Is it possible for me to know it without a doubt? There are a good number of people who hope they are or who guess they might be. The first Christians were in no two minds on the matter. They knew and they had good reasons for their confidence:

● **Jesus has given us his word.** He has promised to forgive and to change those who put their trust in him. We can be completely sure of the promises Jesus makes to us, written in the Bible.

● **What Jesus did for us is complete.** We accept salvation as a gift; we don't have to supplement it with our own efforts. It's not trying – it's trusting.

● **God's Holy Spirit lives in us.** The Holy Spirit leads us into a growing, deepening assurance that we are God's adopted children.

● **Things are different.** We can't explain the changes that have come over us in any other way than that God is doing something in our lives.

● **We belong with other Christians.** We begin to find that we feel more at home with other Christians than with those who don't believe – sometimes even members of our own families.

● **The Bible tells us that God goes on loving us.** In spite of our stumblings and mistakes, and in spite of our changing feelings, God sticks with us. We don't stop being his sons and daughters.

the Christian has to have stamina and keep at it. Praying, obeying, serving, following, resisting, overcoming are all parts of Christian living.

And yet there's more to it than that. For God has pledged himself to us. He completes what he begins. Just as he drew us to him in the first place, he's not going to sit back while we stumble and fall. If Jesus died to save us, he's not going to give us up as easily as that.

The fact is that we need different doses of the truth at different times in our Christian careers. Sometimes we get lazy and let things slide. The Devil trips us up

or we're knocked flying by some sudden misfortune or loss. There are times when we need to be told to get up and get going instead of sitting by the track feeling sorry for ourselves.

But there are other times when the going is wearying, and when our strength seems so small. Those are the times when we're told to look up and remember that the one who saw us through the start will see us across the finishing line. Because when we get there we'll be amazed, not that we persisted with God, but that he persisted with us. We'll admit that it was grace, God's grace, all the way.

10

GOD
SPEAKS!

There's so much uncertainty in the world today – about life and death, about right and wrong, about God and what to believe – that many say they prefer to be agnostics. 'We can't really know,' they argue, 'It could be this – or it could be that. We can't be sure, so we'll keep an open mind.' But if there is a God who made us and who cares for us it stands to reason that he wouldn't leave us in the dark about himself – or even leave us to grope our way to him. We can expect him to show himself to us in various ways, and that is exactly what the Bible claims he has done.

Left in the dark?

Christians believe that God has not left us in the dark about himself. Instead he enjoys letting us know about him. He has left us a permanent record of the way he appeared to people in the past, so that we today can learn from them. Christians believe that the Bible is this permanent record.

The way in which God met with individuals; the way in which he provided for, and disciplined, his people; the particular messages he had for them; the spiritual experiences of those who lived very near to him – all this and more can be found in the pages of the Old Testament, written down and recorded for us over many years and by many different people.

The Jews of Jesus' day had such a respect for the Old Testament that for them it added up to 'the word of God'. They believed that what the Old Testament said, God said. When religious questions came up, it was to the Old Testament that they went for their answers. To be able to quote the writings was the end of the argument.

Jesus himself took the same line. For him too, the Old Testament was God's word. In spite of the new teaching that Jesus gave, he never contradicted the Old Testament. In fact, he said that he had come to fulfil it, to draw out its inner meaning in his teaching, and to live out its predictions and promises in his life, death and resurrection. Those who accept what Jesus said to be true, have to take the Old Testament seriously as well.

The New Testament came together as the first Christians wrote about Jesus' life (the four Gospels), about the early church (Acts), or wrote letters to the young churches. The apostles not only accepted the Old Testament and Jesus' teaching as their guide, they too began to see their own writings on the same level – God revealing himself. They believed that by the power of the Holy Spirit they were speaking on behalf of Christ. Very early on, their writings came to have the same value as the others.

By reading the Bible for ourselves, we can draw on the rich experience many different people have had of God. The Bible tells us all that we need to know about him – and more.

We see something of God in what he's made. Many people are drawn to think of God as they look at nature. The Bible tells us that the creation tells us generally about God's great power and splendour. But for all its wonder and beauty, nature doesn't give us many details about God.

We learn something about God from the way we're made. We are not just things or unthinking creatures. As human beings, we have spiritual needs and ask searching questions about the meaning of life. We can be plagued with our concern about right and wrong. We also feel the need to worship something greater than ourselves. All of these things tell us more about the God who made us in this way. But the picture we get of God only by looking at ourselves is still incomplete and out of focus.

God spoke in history to make himself known. The Old Testament gives us a much clearer picture of God. It tells the story of the nation of Israel, and how he worked in their history. By seeing God in action, encountering people and guiding events, we get to know more about him. But even the Old Testament is incomplete – pointing forward to someone who would show us God more fully.

God finally sent his Son. Jesus gives us the perfect picture of God in his own life. Because he was God, he can show us what God is like – and because he was a man, we can understand him. But Jesus went further. He said that if we want to know God properly, it has to be through him.

The Holy Spirit guided Jesus' followers. The rest of the New Testament completes our understanding about Jesus. Because there were many things about Jesus' life and teaching that his disciples couldn't understand during Jesus' life, God sent his Holy Spirit to teach them about what had happened – and what it all meant. In this way God finished off what he wanted us to know about him. The Bible invites us to go beyond **knowing about** God, to knowing him **for ourselves** in our own experience.

❝These writings bring you back to the living image of that most holy mind, the very Christ himself, speaking, healing, dying, rising . . .❞ Erasmus

God spoke through real people

Some of the Bible's writers went so far as to say that God was speaking directly through them. The Jewish people, and Jesus himself, recognized that this was true. But it would be wrong to think of these writers as a sort of heavenly typing pool with God telling one or another, 'take a letter', or 'write a book'!

When God wanted to make himself known, he took up people and spoke through their personalities, through their times and circumstances, through their background and upbringing. (This is why we need to learn as much as we can about their life and times if we're going to understand what he said.) Although people like Jeremiah said they spoke from God, we still have a pretty good idea from his book what Jeremiah was like too. The same goes for other Bible authors like Hosea, Paul, James or the rest. God was actually using their characters and experiences to teach people what he was like.

Does this mean that the Bible is full of mistakes and human errors? Not if you believe what Jesus said about it. God had such a hand in things that although he allowed the authors to be themselves, he also controlled what they finally put down. That's why Jesus and his followers could go to the Old Testament writings with perfect confidence, and claim that what they had said was what God wanted us to know.

This whole process is called 'inspiration'. Of course, it means more than saying that the Bible is great literature which moves people when they read it – like the works of Shakespeare or Dickens. **It means that God had his hand on its production in such a way that we can accept what we read in the Bible as being completely trustworthy.**

The Bible wasn't written for the privileged few – the rich or the clever. It was written for ordinary people who need direction in their daily lives.

Isn't the Bible out-of-date?

The Bible can seem to be out-of-date when we compare it with many of the modern views and opinions we hear on TV or read about in magazines. Haven't physicists proved finally that God doesn't exist? Hasn't psychology shown that we have created God in our own image? Don't sociologists tell us that all humans need to live in groups, and religions are just one way of doing this?

We need to remember that the physical sciences can only tell us about a physical world. Modern science has helped us to understand our universe better, but to talk about God, who is beyond the physical realm, is outside the scientist's job-description. Many modern scientists do believe in God, and many are Christians.

Psychology and the other human sciences tell us about our needs, but that doesn't mean that there is no reality behind our needs. We have an appetite for food because it exists. And in the same way we could say that we need God because he is there.

The modern view of man as a body and nothing more has not proved popular. People still need to believe that life has purpose and that there is something or someone greater than ourselves. Twentieth-century people can still

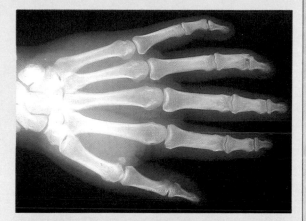

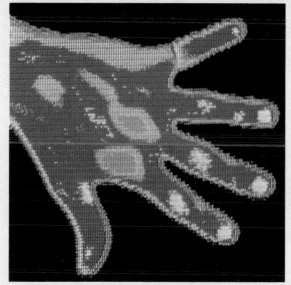

be surprised to start reading the Bible, and find that it rings true to life in their own experience.

An X-ray and a heat picture give us different information about a hand. Science and the Bible give us different views of the world, but both are equally valid.

Are the accounts reliable?

How do we know that what the Bible authors put down was accurate? How do we know that, after all that copying, we have anything like the original books today?

● **The testimony of archaeology.** A good number of Bible stories which used to be dismissed as being impossible have been established as being perfectly accurate simply because of what archaeologists have dug up. A great deal of work has been done in recent years in Palestine and in surrounding countries

which have shown that the Bible accounts are accurate. Many of the historical details in the Bible, like times, places and the way they did things in those days, have come to light through the discoveries which have been made.

Of course, there are many events in the Bible record which we couldn't expect archaeology to 'prove', simply because the people living then didn't leave anything behind which could be unearthed as evidence. But the general background of Bible times is becoming

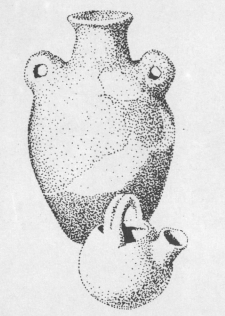

clearer year by year, and what is coming to light strengthens our belief that the Bible authors were very careful when it came to recording what had happened.

● **The evidence of the manuscripts.** Some of the Bible stories weren't written down first of all, but were passed from father to son for several generations. Because of this, some people have argued that all kinds of errors could creep in. But we need to realize that all information was passed along in this way before writing was invented. What is more, we know from primitive tribes who do the same sort of thing today, that it's possible to develop a phenomenal memory for details which we have lost as we rely so much on writing.

Writings, of course, had to be copied by hand before printing came on the scene, and it might be supposed that all sorts of errors could be introduced in that way. Once again, what we know about the way in which the Jews copied their Old Testament simply doesn't support this. They were extremely careful to be accurate, because of the enormous respect for the books themselves. They went out of their way not to make mistakes.

What is more, when it comes to the New Testament, we are more than well off as far as manuscripts are concerned. All that we have of many of the classical writings from Greece or Rome may be just one copy made centuries after the original writing. We have literally hundreds of manuscripts for the New Testament, some containing the whole book, some parts, the earliest of which go back to about two or three hundred years after it was first written. These, together with the early translations into other languages, give us a very good idea of how the New Testament books looked when they were first produced.

Dead Sea Scrolls

One of the most important recent discoveries was the accidental find in the 1940s and 50s of a collection of scrolls which had been written just before or during Jesus' lifetime. Down by the Dead Sea in those days, there was a Jewish monastery where the members spent most of their time studying the Old Testament and adding their own writings to it. Before the Romans destroyed the place around AD 70, the monks hid their library in caves in the area, and there it stayed until an Arab boy stumbled on it. Before this discovery, our oldest manuscript of the Hebrew Old Testament was from about a thousand years after the monks wrote. Because the collection contained Old Testament books, what we know about the text was pushed back about a thousand years almost overnight. One of the interesting results of all this was that the text these monks used was very little different from the one copied down centuries later – which speaks highly of Jewish copying by hand over a thousand years! This can make us even more confident that the Bible is an accurate record of what was originally written.

❝All Scripture is inspired by God and is useful for teaching the truth, rebuking error, correcting faults, and giving instruction for right living . . . ❞ Paul

❝If you believe what you like in the Gospel, and reject what you like, it is not the Gospel you believe, but yourself!❞
Augustine

Who says what's what?

Where do we go for our authority when it comes to what we believe? Over the years even Christians have been divided on this question.

Some people have argued that Jesus entrusted the truth to his church, and that as time has passed and different situations have arisen, the church has had the right to say what's what when it comes to what we believe or how we behave. That's alright as far as it goes, but what happens when the official church begins to speak with a different voice from the Bible? What happens when church teaching actually contradicts the Bible? This is what people like Martin Luther and the other Reformers claimed had happened when they led people back to a faith in the Bible **by itself**.

Others have felt that although Bible teaching might have been alright for the days in which it was written, as we progress in our ideas we must be free to pick and choose, and to discard what doesn't fit with our up-to-date thinking. But who is to say that 'modern thinking' is right and the Bible is wrong? If God has taken the trouble to reveal himself to us, shouldn't we rather test our views in the light of his? This can also lead to a matter of every man for himself. When that happens, we don't end up with what Christians believe, but with a collection of different faiths, each tailored by the individual according to his whims.

The Reformers' view, that the Bible was God's truth for all time, goes back to the belief that Jesus as God's Son was God's last word to us. Because God is a God of truth, he wouldn't contradict himself. He wouldn't tell one generation one thing and another something quite different. History teaches us again and again that fashions in thinking change, and that people have been sincerely wrong in their opinions. We need something outside of our own thinking to keep us on the right track. That's why God gave us the Bible in the first place.

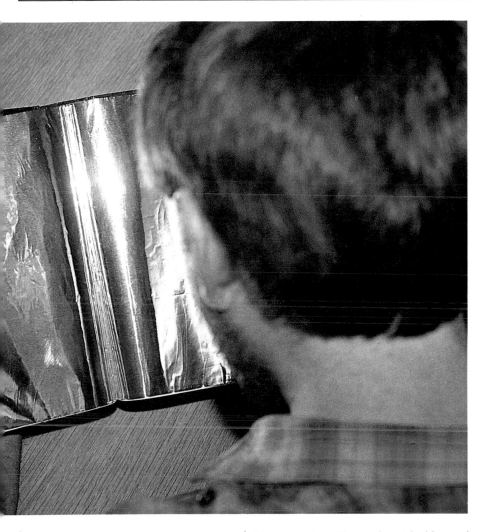

Proving the Bible for ourselves

We can spend a good deal of time talking about the accuracy and reliability of the Bible, of the way in which it is likely that God would speak to mankind and so on, but we'll never really prove the Bible until we face up to its message ourselves.

This is what we do when we first come to faith in Jesus. We believe what the Bible says about him, and we take him at his word, and we discover that things begin to happen in our lives. We prove the truth of the Bible for ourselves. Similar things have taken place whenever the church has placed an emphasis on the Bible as being the word of God. There has been an upsurge of spiritual life as people have proved that God means what he has said.

This is also true as we progress in our

What does the Bible say today?

The Bible was written centuries ago, for people very different from ourselves. But there is a great deal in the Bible which speaks directly to any generation. Our basic needs have not changed, and Christians can still experience the same Holy Spirit who has been working in the lives of men and women from the first Christians right down to today.

But there are still parts of the Bible which don't appear (at first glance, anyway) to have anything to do with us, because they deal with problems we don't face any more. For example, early Christians were very concerned about what they should eat or not eat. This was because Jews who became Christians had been brought up with very strict laws about diet. And also, eating in the pagan world could very easily involve you in the worship of false gods. These problems seem pretty remote from us today.

However, we don't have to cut these chapters out of our Bibles, because in the advice which was given in that situation, there are principles which can apply to very different problems today. Some of the principles in this situation were:
● Christians were not to criticize each other just because they differed over details.

● No Christian was to see himself as spiritually superior to those who didn't do things quite his way.
● Christians were taught to think through what they did, and to be on their guard against simply importing non-Christian standards into the church.
● Above all, they were told that Christians can love one another and yet agree to differ on things which aren't really essential when it comes to living for Christ.

The other difficulty arises when we face a modern

problem about which the Bible says nothing at all. For example, there were no trades unions in those days, and no nuclear weapons. In this sort of case we have to go to the Bible looking for the same timeless principles which apply to our very different needs – things like responsibility, honesty, justice, loyalty, hard work, love for others, a concern for peace. In this way we find that the Bible has a great deal to say to us just where we are today, even though it was written in a very different world from our own.

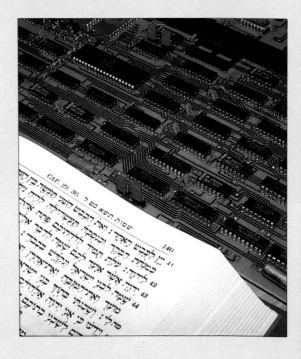

Which Bible translation?

Because language is changing all the time – and because we're discovering more about Bible manuscripts – there can be no final translation of the Bible. Some, like the English King James Version, last for many years because they are so well done – but in order to make the Bible meaningful for ordinary people in our generation, the work of translation must go on.

English-speaking people have a wide range of Bible translations, some close to the original text, others trying to capture the liveliness of modern English, but all useful when it comes to introducing people to Bible reading.

● For someone who is just starting out in the Bible, the *Living Bible* might be extremely helpful.
● For general reading in up-to-date English, try the *Good News Bible*, or *J. B. Phillips'* translation of the New Testament.
● For a good study of the Bible text, use something like the *Revised Standard Version*, the *New International Version*, or the *New American Standard Version*.

In some parts of the world, however, local languages have never been reduced to writing, let alone used for a Bible translation. Many Christian translators use modern methods of language study and give their time and energy to developing written languages and translating the Bible into them. The motive behind such hard work is that everybody has the right to hear and to read the good news about Jesus in their own language. And when they do, they too can prove for themselves what he can accomplish in their lives.

Christian living. This is why it is so important that, having become Christians, we begin to read the Bible for ourselves. There is so much that God wants us to know about himself, about ourselves, and about what he can do for us if only we let him. Many Christians have discovered that by setting aside time from their daily programme to read the Bible and to pray, they have begun to see everything they do in a new light. Of course, this is not always possible for everyone because of jobs or circumstances. There are no rigid 'rules' about reading the Bible. But we will find it a great strength to read and understand the Bible. After all, if the Bible is God's word – God speaking to us – then as we read and absorb it we will actually begin to think God's thoughts after him. We begin to see the world and its needs as he does. And we begin to see the possibilities in our own lives when God is let into the picture.

11

IN IT
TOGETHER

What a mess! At least, that's what we might be tempted to think when we look at the church today – and even more so if we study a bit of its history. Different groups and denominations argue with one another. Some seem to be up to their ears in undesirable political activities like the 'Protestants' and 'Catholics' in Northern Ireland, or the Phalangist 'Christians' in Lebanon. Some dress, act and speak as though they had just stepped out of the Middle Ages. From another angle, the church seems irrelevant to what is going on all around us. Decaying buildings, musty hymn books, deadly singing and boring sermons are all that some associate with the word 'church'. Did Jesus really intend to found this?

And yet the Bible teaches that God's plan for getting people right with himself, a plan decided before the beginning of time, comes to focus in the church. Perhaps we ought to take another look and ask ourselves what it means by this.

God deals with groups

It's true that each person must get right with God himself or herself. No one can believe for you – it's your own affair. But having said that, we mustn't forget that there's another dimension to human life. We belong together. That's the way God made us, and that's the way God deals with us.

In the Old Testament, God called Abraham to follow him, but not just so that he could bless Abraham – he had an eye to his descendants as well. Moses stands out too, as do people like David and Elijah and Jeremiah, but they all operated within the framework of God's chosen nation, Israel.

Jesus did a similar thing. He didn't just work alone, but chose an inner circle of twelve followers to learn from him and to get the message out. After he left and the Spirit came, this little group began to grow fantastically, thousands being added to its number. The church had been born.

What is the church?

Paul described the togetherness of the human race as being 'in Adam'. By birth we are all tied up together with him, inheriting the disabling effects of what he did. In the same breath, however, Paul is also prepared to speak about Jesus as the second or last Adam, someone who

The church is people – God's People – not just buildings, denominations, structures or organizations. The church can exist without any of these, for wherever there are believing people, there is the church.

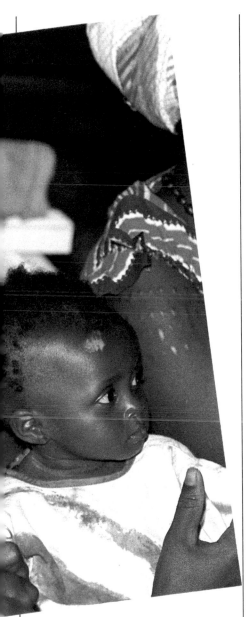

The New Testament uses several pictures of the church to help us understand what it is. No one picture gives us the full truth, but together they show up what God intends his church to be like.

● **A body.** Just as the various parts of the human body work together, so everyone in the church makes different contributions, but in unity. Jesus, like the head of a body, gives the church its direction and life.

● **Christ's bride.** Paul says that Christ loves the church and gave up his life for her. Because of this, God's people are called to be morally pure and wholly given over to Jesus.

● **God's temple.** In the Old Testament, the Jerusalem Temple was the place where God was present. The church is God's temple, not built with bricks and mortar, but with the living stones of committed men and women. God is present among his people the church, and he is active by his Holy Spirit.

● **A royal priesthood.** Priests in the Old Testament provided a bridge between the people and God. Because all Christians are adopted children of God, they all have direct access to him through Jesus Christ.

● **Lights in a dark world.** Each local church represents Jesus and his message like a candle in the night. This attracts other people to new life through him.

The New Testament tells us clearly that Jesus meant to start the church – it wasn't an invention by the first Christians. His church is a permanent feature of our world until Jesus returns to end all history.

would head up a new race, the company of those who are being re-made through Christ. This new humanity is expressed in the church.

❝I will build my church, and not even death will ever be able to overcome it.❞ Jesus

Why so many denominations?

Outsiders looking at the churches today are often bewildered by the number of different groups all competing, it seems, with one another. If the church really is supposed to be one, how did this happen?

● **Some divisions are sincere differences of opinion.** Some differences concern issues that don't seem all that important, like the way the church is organized, or the form that worship takes. But these differences should not be underestimated. It would be difficult to combine a Quaker service (where silence is kept) with a joyful, noisy Pentecostal service! Other differences are much more fundamental, and concern questions of belief. Big differences divide Protestantism, Roman Catholicism and the Orthodox churches.

● **Some differences are accidents of history.** When Martin Luther began to preach and teach the Bible, his aim was not to launch the Reformation churches, but to reform the Roman Catholic church. But he was forced out of Roman Catholicism. Methodism came into being because the Church of England could not cope with the large numbers of converts which were the result of the preaching of Wesley and others.

● **Many differences do not really matter at all.** When it comes to the central issue of believing in Jesus Christ and living for him, many Christians from all the traditions discover that they have a great deal in common –

even though they might express it in different ways.

Over the years, attempts have been made to bring the different groups together so that there might be one church and not many. The aim of the Ecumenical Movement is to get members of different denominations talking and working together, and this in turn has led, in some instances, to denominations merging with one another.

While this concern and work for unity is good, there are others who feel that this is only papering over the cracks. They say there must be a real basis of shared belief if there is going to be any real unity. That is why, even before the Ecumenical Movement came on the scene, those who shared a common belief in the authority of the Bible felt it possible to co-operate, especially when it came to preaching the good news. While allowing for a variety of different types of worship and church organization, they have achieved a great deal in terms of evangelism at home and mission overseas.

If we are going to be one in heaven in spite of our denominational differences, it makes sense if we make a start here and now. This means that we'll go out of our way to try to understand those who worship differently from us. We'll respect them as Christian believers and members of the same family, even though they might organize themselves in a different way. We'll do our best to share with them – prepared to learn from them as well as giving to them. We'll explore ways and means of working together, especially when it comes to sharing Jesus with people who still haven't heard the good news.

The different denominations show us the rich variety of ways people worship God.

The new sharing

When people became Christians in those early days, they discovered a wonderful thing which we can discover today as well. They had something deep and fundamental in common with all other believers everywhere. **The same Holy Spirit lived in each person.** They all shared in him, and because of that they shared in many other things too. This sharing (which is what the word 'fellowship' means) was therefore something which God gave them. Although at times they needed reminding of its practical outworkings, they didn't need to be taught it. In the same way, if we belong to Jesus, we will feel at one with any other Christians, wherever they may be and whatever their background.

The apostle Paul spoke of the church as a body where all the parts work together in harmony.

We see this at the very beginning when the first Christians expressed their oneness by sharing their possessions, and living out of a common fund. From the New Testament letters we can see that their sharing was an intensely practical affair. They shared in worship; they shared their cash; they shared their leaders. They shared their homes, their needs and the work of spreading the good news about Jesus. Their sharing on earth was just a foretaste of what things would be like in heaven.

The church is a family, and all those who have been born again belong to one another. This is why the New Testament told the first Christians – and tells us – to welcome, to accept and to put up with one another. We are to love one another, forgive those who hurt us, carry each other's burdens, encourage and build one another up. And all because of the way in which God our Father has dealt with us. Loving, after all, is the family likeness

which people ought to see among God's children.

Worshipping together

Although Christians do many other things together, they feel especially at home with one another when they worship God. As in the early church, worship today has many ingredients:

● **We come together to praise and thank God** for who he is and for what he's done for us. He's opened our eyes to the fact that we owe literally everything that's good to him. Not only our material possessions, not only our physical health and well-being, but our very existence, for we were made for him. Most of all we recognize what it cost him – and his Son – to bring us back to him.

● **We sadly have to admit that we have failed him.** In spite of the strength God gives us, we all too often let him down in the ways that we speak and think, in the ways that we act and react. So we come confessing our sins, knowing that they stand in the way. For if we are to worship properly, we must be right with God. Because of what Jesus did, God wonderfully reassures us that he accepts us and fully forgives us.

● **We bring our needs to him.** He has invited us to pray for one another, especially for those who are sick or in special need. But our prayers don't stop with the group, because we're also aware of the needs of those outside – not just their material or social needs, but the fact that many have never known the joy of being right with God.

● **We listen to what he has to say.** We read the Bible together, and we listen to those to whom God has given something for the whole church. Sometimes God speaks through the experience of others as they share with us what he has been doing with them. He has also specially equipped some to explain and apply

Bible truths for us.

● **We remember what he has done for us,** and we reaffirm our faith in him. This is why Jesus told his disciples to eat bread and drink wine together to celebrate the Lord's Supper or Communion. But in many other ways we remind each other of his love, his goodness and his power.

● **We remind ourselves that he is Lord.** We pledge ourselves to live for Jesus in ordinary, everyday life. We give in to him as he points out areas in our experience which are uncommitted. We ask for his strength to be what we profess to be – not only when we're with other Christians, but as we face the crises, the strains and stresses, and the humdrum round of living in a fallen world as Christ's representatives. For worship must carry over into life.

We do all these things in a variety of ways. We may sing hymns or choruses; or sometimes choirs or groups of individuals will lead us in worship through song. We may use a set pattern of praise and prayer; we may have a free, unstructured service. We may bring our gifts as part of our self-giving. The actual service will be different from one church to the next, or even from one Sunday to the next. **But the important thing is that we come together to worship, to draw near to God and to spend time with him as his people together. And we know that when we do this, it delights and pleases him as much as the affection of children delights and pleases parents.**

Pooling our resources

Nobody can do everything. God gives different gifts to different people. It is our responsibility to work as a team, sharing what we've got.

The Bible tells us that the Holy Spirit is actively at work in the church. He

What are baptism and communion?

BAPTISM

Jesus himself was baptized in the river Jordan by John, and he instructed his disciples to baptize all who wanted to follow him. In the story of the earliest churches, we find them doing just this. When people responded to the good news, they expressed their commitment to Christ by being baptized. That's what being baptized 'in his name' means: we are now his property.

Christians have often disagreed about who Jesus intended to be baptized, and how it should be done. Many hold that the children of believers may be baptized, because it is hoped that one day they will come to faith in Christ too. Others maintain that baptism only makes sense if you are a believer at the time. Again, some use little water, sprinkling or pouring it over the head of the person being baptized. Others argue that it should involve being immersed in water.

Certainly, in the New Testament, baptism marked the beginning of Christian life and experience. It is a picture of washing, or forgiveness. There is nothing magical about it, because Christ forgives us only when we confess our sins and trust in him. Because it marked the start of a Christian's life, it was also the way in which people joined the church.

THE LORD'S SUPPER

On the night before he died, Jesus had supper with his disciples, quite possibly celebrating the Passover Meal when the Jews remembered their deliverance from Egypt. Jesus took the bread and wine, and told his friends that they represented his body (which would be hung on a cross for them) and his blood (which would be shed for them). What's more, he told them to remember his death in this way, eating and drinking together until he returned for them.

Just as the Passover meal acted out what had happened on the night when the Jews left Egypt, Christians were to relive with bread and wine the night when Jesus was betrayed.

How this is done today, and what the meal is called, varies by denomination. Sometimes it is referred to as communion (which means fellowship), or the breaking of bread, the mass, or the eucharist (which means thanksgiving). The important thing to remember is that it represents our ongoing life with Christ. Just as we need meals to keep us alive, we need to be continually drawing on Christ's strength to live for him daily. It also reminds us that, one day, the struggle will be over when Jesus returns to wind up history and to finish off the work he has begun in us. Then the church – as well as individual Christians – will be what it was meant to be.

How to run the church

Different churches are organized and run in different ways. But there are four main kinds of church government:

● **Rule from the top,** where church leaders (often called bishops) take decisions for a group of churches in a particular area. Authority is centralized, although below the bishops are lower orders of clergy who look after individual churches. Examples of this system would be the Anglican and Episcopalian churches, the Roman Catholic, Lutheran and Orthodox churches. Methodism is a modified variety, while some of the more recent independent house churches organize themselves on similar lines.

● **All ministers are equal** in the Presbyterian system, taking their places alongside elders in the churches and running them together. The churches co-operate with one another, usually both at an area and at a national level.

● **The people must decide,** as far as Baptists, Congregationalists and many independent Free Churches are concerned. They believe that God guides each individual group of Christians as they prayerfully meet together. In this way, they appoint church officers to look after the general running of church affairs, and invite the person whom they feel to be right as their minister.

● **Everyone has a share in the work** of the church in Brethren Assemblies, and all the men are free to take part in the services. Although the pattern varies from place to place, they do not usually have a minister, but senior men are recognized as elders. These look after the general leadership and pastoral care of the fellowship.

gives a wide range of special abilities to different Christians. Some are able to speak; others are able to run things. Some are particularly good at sharing the good news with non-Christians; others are great encouragers. Some have gifts that can be used especially in worship; some are particularly used in healing; others work behind the scenes, helping, giving and serving. **The important thing to notice is that everyone is expected to be involved.**

But it was also recognized in the Bible that God does give some people special gifts which enable them to take a lead in the churches and particularly to preach and teach. In many churches these people are given the responsibility of looking after God's people.

The way in which these particular leadership gifts have been used over the years has varied from church to church. Some leaders are specially set apart to get on with their job (usually called 'ordination'). Other leaders are simply recognized by a church as having special God-given abilities. However it is arranged, every local church recognizes in one way or another that they need God-given leadership.

But there's a great deal of difference between church leadership and, for example, political leadership. Church leaders should not be 'the boss' – throwing their weight around and telling everyone what to do. Instead, they are servants of the church. This is the pattern Jesus himself set. At the last meal before his death, he did a slave's job – he washed his disciples' feet! That is the humble path he calls church leaders to follow today.

The church in the world

The church was never intended as a cosy club for Christians. It lives in the world and can often be unpopular because it stands for Jesus. The church is in the world for a reason – so how does it relate to those outside?

● **Separate from the world.** The church needs to keep clear of the world's sinful attitudes. Christians have a new set of standards and values which they apply to life, and these are radically different from the way non-Christians do things. The church is God's new society. This means that our relationships and behaviour towards each other will be changed. As we share our lives (and even, perhaps, our possesions) with each other, other people will be attracted to Jesus.

● **Involved in society.** Jesus said Christians were like salt (which was used in those days as an antiseptic to stop the rot) and like light, letting people see by our lifestyle that we have something better. This is why the church must be involved in the world, not in some small corner. The church can show it cares by reaching out to meet the physical needs of men and women. In this way it continues the work Jesus did during his life.

● **Supports justice and freedom.** The church prays and works for a peaceful and just society. Human laws are one of the ways in which God works to restrain evil in a fallen world. It is only when laws demand that we deny our faith, or compromise our Christian standards, that we should dig our heels in and refuse to obey them for the sake of Christ.

● **Speaks to society.** The church can

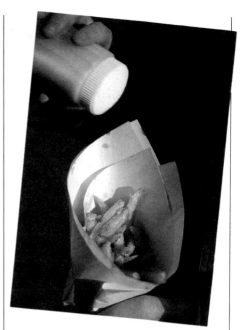

❝You are like salt for all mankind.❞
Jesus to his disciples

especially speak out when society decides to do something which is clearly contrary to God's will. How much voice it has will depend on the political system in power. In democracies, the church has plenty of opportunities to make its views known.

● **Spreads the good news.** As a church we are called actively and vigorously to tell people about Jesus and what he has done. We do this by speaking the good news and by living it for ourselves in the heart of our world.

12

FACING THE FUTURE

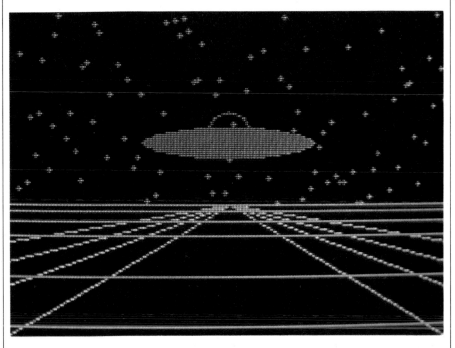

Futurology – guessing what is going to happen in the next hundred years or so – has become a refined art-form among the experts. Reading the trends, watching the statistics, calculating the rate at which we are using up our resources, weighing up the risks of calamity takes up a good deal of some people's time. And it's all big business, because of the times we live in.

Our planet is threatened with runaway overpopulation, the fine balance of nature is being upset by pollution, and we can now unleash a terrifying fire of destruction which would quite literally spell the end of all life on earth.

Is that the way it's going to end? The human race committing suicide? Or is God, who made this world, going to write the last chapter in its history?

The Jewish people at the time of Jesus split history into two ages. The present age, in which there was evil and suffering, would end when the Messiah came. Then there would be no more pain or sin.

THE AGE TO COME

THIS AGE

The Messiah's coming

The ages overlap

The Jews knew that this world is going somewhere, and that there is a purpose in history. They divided the whole of history into two ages – this age and the age to come. This age is fallen, sinful and will pass away; the age to come is God's age, when men and women will live on a renewed earth as they were intended to. What's more they believed that the age to come will be ushered in by the coming King, the promised Messiah. This is what they were looking for in Jesus' day. What they didn't realize was that Messiah had to come a first time to live and die for us. Even Jesus' disciples didn't see that until he had risen from the dead.

But if Jesus is the Messiah and has come, then the age to come has also come! By the Holy Spirit, the New Testament tells us, Christians may already taste the life of the new age here and now – that's what is meant by eternal life. But the old age hasn't come to an end yet. It's still going on. Men and women in this fallen world are just as fallen. Has something gone wrong with God's scheme?

No, because he intended the two ages to overlap for a while. **Christians are living in that overlap – in two ages at once. At one level they have to face all the rough and tumble of a fallen world. They have to cope with temptation and suffering like the rest. They know illness and death – but they also begin to live in the new age as soon as they put their trust in Jesus and receive his Holy Spirit.** In that way, they have something on account, a bit of heaven within them here and now, which makes them look up and away from the present scene to the day when Jesus will return for them. That will be when the old world order will come to an end. The old age will terminate – but the new age will go on in all its unhindered glory and delight.

But the first Christians came to believe that these two ages overlapped. The old age, with its bad effects, continues, but God's rule on earth has already begun. The old age will only end when Jesus returns to bring history to its conclusion.

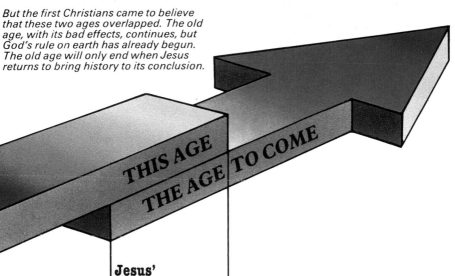

THIS AGE

THE AGE TO COME

Jesus' first coming   **Jesus' return**

Life after death

When the writer Arthur Koestler died as the result of a suicide pact with his wife, he wistfully recorded in his will the hope that there might be some vague, impersonal after-life, an existence out of the body. In doing this he was reflecting an age-old belief that this life is not all that there is, and that death is not the end.

For thousands of years people of all races have believed in some sort of life after death. Even the most primitive peoples often have very elaborate funeral rituals because of this. And the Pharaohs of ancient Egypt packed their tombs with their favourite possesions for use in the after-life.

For most ancient peoples death was not a welcome affair. Life after death was seen as either this life continued, or more often as a shadowy, gloomy business. But it was life of a sort after death. It is modern people, with their materialistic view of life, who have argued themselves out of this belief. Because they believe that they are no more than bodies, life ends once and for all at death. Or does it?

The widespread interest in the possibility of something more than this life tells us that people don't find the argument too satisfying. This is why spiritualists, who claim to be able to make contact with the world of the dead, thrive in our twentieth century world as they did in the past. This is why we are fascinated by accounts of 'out of the body' experiences by those who have clinically died and been resuscitated.

But although this kind of 'evidence' can be very interesting, it doesn't prove anything. Just to want something badly enough doesn't mean that we're going to get it. A longing for life after death may just be wishful thinking. Our ordinary, natural knowledge ends with death. If there is anything beyond it, it would need to be shown to us – and that's exactly what we find in the Bible.

Most people are fascinated – or frightened – by the future. The Bible gives us solid reasons to look forward to the future with hope.

New bodies for a new life

What do Christians believe about life after death?

We need bodies to be complete human beings and that's what we will get when Jesus returns. He will give us new bodies, perfectly adapted to the life of the new age. Jesus himself had a real human body after his resurrection, and this is seen in the Bible as the prototype of ours.

However, when we study the way he appeared (and disappeared), we begin to realize that his resurrection body was rather different from our present, physical bodies.

These bodies wear out – our new bodies won't. These bodies are often weak, especially as we get older – our new bodies will give us powers that we never had before. These bodies carry the marks of a fallen world on them – our new bodies will be fitted for sharing Christ's glory in the new age.

The Bible shows us Jesus, who not only taught about life after death, but died himself and came back to tell us about it! The central fact of the good news is that Jesus has broken the power of death once and for all – and that those who trust him can face it without fear or anxiety.

> **❝ I am the resurrection and the life. Whoever believes in me will live, even though he dies; and whoever lives and believes in me will never die. Do you believe this? ❞**
>
> Jesus

Re-entry

Christians believe that we have not seen the last of Jesus. The Bible says that he will return to our planet to conclude human history as we now know it. This event is closely tied to our hope in new life after death. There is no mistaking the Bible's teaching about Christ's return to earth:

● **He will come in person.** It will be Jesus himself, recognized by everyone. We can't explain the second coming away in terms of some vague movement or force for good in the world. It will be a definite event.

● **It will be seen by all.** Everybody will be aware of the fact when it happens. We're not sure how – but more than once the Bible tells us how surprised everybody will be when they're suddenly confronted with the truth about Jesus.

● **It will be wonderful.** No birth in a cattle stall this time. We'll see Jesus as he really is – Son of God, rightful Lord of the universe, in all his power and majesty.

● **The opposition will melt away.** Instead of people's proud boasting that they can get along without God or Christ, everyone will stand silenced and open-mouthed. The powerful forces of evil will be overthrown simply by Christ appearing.

● **It will mark the end.** For Christ will come to judge and to reign. It will be God's way of saying to a rebellious world, 'enough!' And this present, wicked age will finally be wound up.

State visit

The word the New Testament writers used for Jesus' return meant just that. It described an official visit to a particular city by the emperor or some high state official. When the person in question got near to the place, all the citizens would stream out and line the road to welcome his party, falling in behind them and bringing him in through the gates with great pomp and rejoicing. We're told in the Bible that, in a similar way, when Jesus comes back, Christians will meet him and join in with his triumphant re-entry.

Thief in the night

No burglar ever sent you a postcard to tell you when he was going to break into your home. We usually discover that he's been and gone after the event. That's the picture Jesus and his disciples used when they wanted to tell us how unexpected his return would be. But the warning means that at least some will be ready for it.

Doomwatch with a difference

The days are gone when people thought that this world would go on for ever with everything getting better all the time. Our scientists, ecologists, economists and international observers are predicting that the human race will finally rub itself out in one of half a dozen ways. The only question seems to be how long can we delay the inevitable.

There's really nothing new about this though. Jesus told us that the world would end, but with a difference. It would not be an accident. God would end it when Jesus came back to close this present evil age and to preside in judgement. The whole period between Jesus' resurrection and his return to earth is called 'the last days' in the Bible. Jesus told us what to expect in this period.

● **Evil in society.** Human nature will come out in its true colours. Selfishness, greed, injustice, deception and perversion – all the marks of moral anarchy – are predicted in the Bible before Jesus returns. A glance at our present world and its horrors underlines this.

● **International friction.** Instead of our naive dream of international peace and co-operation, there will be wars and struggles. National pride and greed, the stupidity of politicians and the belligerence of generals will threaten international relations.

● **Widespread religious error.** Superstitions and faiths which contradict the teaching of the Bible will become popular. Many people who profess to be Christians will also be taken in. But a nucleus of Christians worldwide will remain faithful to God.

● **Fierce persecution.** Christians who are prepared to hang on and to stand out from the rest will be given a rough ride. They will be contradicted, bullied, denied employment – even imprisoned, tortured and killed unless they give up their beliefs. Persecutions have happened like this ever since Jesus died. But martyrdom isn't just history. It has been reckoned that there have been more martyrs in this generation than in any since the early days of the church.

● **Cosmic upheavals.** Jesus predicted that before he returned there would be disasters and natural calamities on earth. He also said that strange sights would be seen in the heavens. As mankind and the world are closely connected, it's not surprising if our blatant sinning has an effect on creation itself.

● **The Jewish people.** Although our data is limited, there is enough in the Bible to tell us that God has a future for his ancient people, Israel. Towards the end of history we are told that they will turn back to God. Some Christians think

that the Bible also predicts a return to their own land.

● **The good news will be heard.** In spite of the opposition, men and women will carry the message of Jesus to people everywhere. The modern missionary movement has been reaching out for nearly 200 years now with the aim that everybody, everywhere should hear about Jesus.

● **A world dictator.** He's called the Antichrist in the New Testament because he will claim the sort of honour and worship which only Christ deserves. Just as evil men like Hitler or Stalin have rapidly and cleverly risen to power in the past, and have been followed blindly by millions of people, so also this man will appear on the world scene, backed by Satan and bent on everything that is evil.

If you read the words of Jesus and his followers and study current affairs you will have to admit that all the ingredients are there already. We are living with a cosmic time-bomb. What Jesus didn't tell us was precisely when it would finally blow up.

Final reckoning

Jesus is coming back as judge. When he does the books will be opened and each person will have to account for the way he or she has lived on earth. Although there is a sense in which God judges human beings here and now – especially in the chaos they bring upon themselves by their own sinful idiocy – it is only at the end that the accounts will finally be squared. And we're told more than once that, on that great day, Jesus will act for his Father as our judge.

Because of this we know that it will be absolutely fair. And because God sees everything, all the evidence will be taken into account. Jesus will take into consideration not only what people have done, but also why they have done it. Their motives will be as important on judgement day as their actions. He will a▮▮▮▮ge us according to what we know of good and evil. Those who have a fuller knowledge of what God wants will have more to answer for.

Everyone will be involved in God's judgement. Christians who are already aquitted because of Jesus' death for them must still answer for the way they've used their resources in serving or not serving Christ. Those who are not Christians and who have rejected God will find that he has rejected them. God will simply agree with the choice they have made – and this choice will be final. That is why it is so important that we take God's offer of forgiveness and life here and now.

But judgement is not simply a terrifying event. Christians can look forward to it with great hope, because there everyone will see God's justice. Evil will be expelled, the Devil and sin will be destroyed for good, and we will enter in to enjoy the presence of our God. It will be the time when suffering and grief finally come to an end, and when God will receive the praise that is rightly his.

What about hell?

People today might be amazed that many Christians still believe in a literal hell. How could a loving God allow such a chamber of horrors to exist – let alone send people to it? No one enjoys believing in hell – and yet the fact remains that Jesus and his followers said a great deal about it. What can we learn from what they said?

● **Hell is simply to be cut off from God.** The Bible uses many different pictures about hell, but the important thing to remember is that hell is life without God. Many people say that they don't want God to interfere with the way they run their lives. It seems that hell is the place where this wish comes dreadfully true.

● **Hell doesn't just happen to us.** In this life we get ready for the future life. By following Jesus now we get ready to live with God. By refusing God now we get ready to live without him for ever.

● **Hell is the end of everything good.** Some people think of hell like a teenage party that really gets going once the parents have left. But without God, life becomes nothing. All the good things we enjoy – love, laughter, friendship – will vanish in hell.

● **Hell grieves God.** God doesn't want people to reject all that he has to give and he weeps over the tragic waste of human lives. But he also respects our freedom to choose who we are for ourselves. In the end, it is we who decide for or against hell.

● **Hell is a warning for us now.** The reason Jesus spoke so often and so vividly about God's punishment of evil was to warn us to avoid it. He did this not to terrify us about God, but because he loves us and wants the best for us.

● **Hell was why Jesus died.** When we see what Jesus went through for us on the cross, we can only conclude that he was trying to rescue us from something dreadful. We would be foolish not to accept his free offer of life here and now.

Heaven on earth

The Bible doesn't give us a complete picture of heaven. But it does give us some tantalizing glimpses of the life we will enjoy with God and his people. Heaven is not a vague place, with clouds and harps. The Bible promises that God will recreate the earth and that we will live with him on it. Heaven will be on earth, where we feel perfectly at home – with Jesus and with each other. For heaven will be a place of meeting and enjoying relationships.

At the heart of this new life will be God himself. We will see Jesus in all his glory – and we will share that glory with him. Whatever people think of us here, there we will be shown to be what we really are, sons and daughters of God himself. To be with Jesus will be heaven enough.

Seeing the Lord like this is the ultimate human experience. It is what we were made for, and difficult to describe. If a beautiful view or a deep friendship can thrill us beyond words here and now, seeing Jesus as he is will be everything we could ever want.

We will see him and know him perfectly, because there won't be any sin in heaven, nor will there be any of the worldly distractions which often make it so hard for us to maintain our link with him. That's why heaven will also be a place of worship at its purest and highest.

God's work in us will be complete. We will perfectly reflect Christ's beauty and in that way we will be fully and finally remade as God originally designed us – in his image. We will leave behind the struggles and battles of this life here. That is why heaven is sometimes pictured as rest or relaxation. It is not perpetual idleness, but a rest of heart and mind which we now experience only briefly. No wonder then that heaven will be a happy place. There will be no more tears or sighing or groaning. The Jews pictured heaven as a marvellous meal together with the Messiah, where everybody would enjoy themselves to the full.

We will be together. It is natural that we will recognize one another, and enjoy heaven in the company of those with whom we've shared the struggles and burdens of this life. What is more, it will be permanent. No more partings. A lasting home in contrast with so much that Christians have to endure in this age.

Life between the times

What we've been looking at is too good to keep to ourselves. That's why Jesus' last command was to go out into the wide world and share the good news with everyone everywhere – and that command still stands. But there aren't many commands like that in the Bible – there don't have to be. God's good news is naturally infectious. As we are filled with the life and power of Jesus, so it will spill over to those around us. Our faith was made to be shared.

Jesus and his followers didn't teach about the future so that we could give up on the present. On the contrary, what we look forward to should make us better Christians here and now.

For those who are going through great difficulties and suffering, the future is a tremendous comfort and encouragement. One day we'll see that it was all worth it. And what lies ahead helps us to lift our hearts and our heads, and get on with the job we have to do in this world.

But on the other hand, it is also a stimulus. Jesus may come back at any time. That automatically poses the question, 'Will we be ready when he comes?' We can only be sure by living for him in the present. Then we will be able to face him unashamed whenever he might appear. Then we will really look forward to his return.

At the end of the summer, farmers harvest their crops. Jesus used this picture of bringing home the grain to describe the end of the world.

66 We shall rest and we shall see, we shall see and we shall love, we shall love and we shall pray, in the end which is no end. **99**

Augustine

Acknowledgements

The photographs in this book have been
supplied by ZEFA Limited. Additional
photographs and drawings are
reproduced by permission of the
following individuals and agencies:

Barnaby's Picture Library, 110, 118
Simon Bull, 98, 99
John Chillingworth, 108
Church Missionary Society, 106–7
Fritz Fankhauser, 15
Sonia Halliday Photographs/Sister
    Daniel, 29/Sonia Halliday, 58/Barry
    Searle, 52/Jane Taylor, 48–49, 109
Alan Hutchison Library, 43, 53, 63
Lion Publishing, 32, 37, 102/
    Simon Jenkins, 91 /Brooke Snell, 23,
    40, 66, 82, 100–101, 112, 114/Jon
    Willcocks, 24–25, 31, 62, 125
Picturepoint, 6–7, 74–75, 80–81
Jean-Luc Ray, 78, 108
Science Photo Library, 97
Doug Sewell, 70
United Artists Corporation, 'Audrey
    Rose', 46
Liam White, 109